TOM SAWYER

a play in four acts

by
PAUL KESTER

founded on the story of the same name
by Samuel L. Clemens

SAMUEL FRENCH, INC.
45 West 25th Street   New York 10010
7623 Sunset Boulevard   Hollywood 90046
LONDON   TORONTO

The following is a copy of program of the first performance of "TOM SAWYER" as presented at the Alvin Theatre, New York, December 25, 1931:

THE NATIONAL JUNIOR THEATRE

Presents

TOM SAWYER

A Comedy in Four Acts

Dramatized by Paul Kester from the story
by Samuel L. Clemens
Staged by Katherine Brown and Glenna Tinnin

CAST OF CHARACTERS

WIDOW DOUGLAS .... *Kate Conway*
AUNT POLLY .... *Alice John*
MRS. HARPER .... *Dorothy Stewart*
WALTER POTTER .... *William Lovejoy*
MARY ROGERS .... *Mary Cullinan*
DR. ROBINSON .... *George Lee*
BECKY THATCHER .... *Mary Buckner*
SID SAWYER .... *Ezra Stone*
MUFF POTTER .... *Melvin Fox*
GRACIE MILLER .... *Katherine Rolin*
TOM SAWYER .... *Preston Dawson, Jr.*
JOE HARPER .... *Robert de Lany*
INJUN JOE .... *John Shellie*
BEN ROGERS .... *William L. Keen*
HUCKLEBERRY FINN .... *Clifford Adams*
ALFRED TEMPLE .... *Adelbert Stephenson*
AMY LAWRENCE .... *Frances Fulton*
REVEREND SPRAGUE .... *Richard Enbach*
SHERIFF JONES .... *Arthur de Angelis*
JUDGE THATCHER .... *L'Estrange Millman*
MRS. THATCHER

SCENES

ACT I. *The Village Street. Late afternoon. Monday.*
ACT II. *The Village School. Tuesday morning.*
ACT III. *Aunt Polly's house. Saturday night.*
ACT IV. SCENE I. *Jackson's Island. Before dawn. Sunday.*
        SCENE II. *The Village Street. Sunday morning.*

DESCRIPTION OF CHARACTERS

BECKY *is a pretty little girl with curls down her back, her ruffled pantalettes show under her short skirt.*

SID *is about ten or twelve.*

WALTER POTTER *is a young man, resolute and rather stern of aspect.*

INJUN JOE *is dark and evil-looking, poorly but not raggedly dressed.*

AUNT POLLY *is a middle-aged woman with a sharp but kindly visage.*

GRACIE MILLER *is a shrewish little girl with neglected hair and shabby dress.*

TOM SAWYER *is barefoot and one toe is tied up in a white rag.*

BEN ROGERS *is a boy of about* TOM'S *size, barefoot.*

HUCKLEBERRY FINN *is a boy of about* TOM'S *size and age but ragged and unkempt. His coat trails behind him almost to the ground, his long trousers are rolled up and fastened by one suspender, his hat is a ruin, and he is barefoot.*

MUFF POTTER *is careless and neglected in dress, his appearance that of the village drunkard. About fifty years old.*

JOE HARPER *is about* TOM'S *age. Has a bladder attached to a string in his hand.*

ALFRED TEMPLE *is an offensive, citified boy; wears shoes, a natty hat and a necktie.*

The other Characters will be found fully described in the book on which this play is founded.

TOM SAWYER

ACT ONE

SCENE: *The village street.*

Down Right is seen AUNT POLLY'S *house with its wing and shed. A board fence shuts in the yard. The gate is immediately before the door at* R. *The fence runs off* R.I.

Down L. *is* DR. ROBINSON'S *office, a low, white frame building with steps leading from the door* L. *to the sidewalk. The window opens on the side toward the street at* L.I. *There is a sign above the door supported by a strong iron bracket.*

Above the doctor's office is the path leading to the HARPER *house, which is set back in a yard with a fence and gate before it.*

At back C. *the Village Church is seen with broad steps leading up to its front doors.*

At Rise of Curtain the WIDOW DOUGLAS, MRS. HARPER *and* MRS. THATCHER *come from the* HARPER *house at* L. *and pause at the gate.*

MRS. DOUGLAS. Now you both bring your sewing and come up and spend the day at Cardiff Hill real soon.

(As MRS. DOUGLAS *speaks* BECKY THATCHER *enters from* R.U. *with* SID. BECKY *is a pretty little girl with curls down her back, her ruffled pan-*

7

talettes show under her short skirt. SID *is about
ten or twelve. He crosses to* AUNT POLLY'S
house at R.I, *carrying his books.)*

SID. Goodby, Becky. See you after 'while. *(Exit*
SID *into* AUNT POLLY'S *house.)*

BECKY. *(Crossing to* HARPER *gate)* School's out,
and oh!—I wasn't scared a bit. May I go play with
Amy Lawrence now? We sat in school together.

MRS. THATCHER. Yes, dear—but don't be gone
too long. Run in and put your books away before
you go. *(Exit* BECKY *into* HARPER *house.)*

MRS. DOUGLAS. *(Looking after her)* I wish
you'd let me have your Becky——

MRS. THATCHER. I reckon you'd have to speak to
Judge Thatcher about that.

MRS. DOUGLAS. I know what he'd say. My house
did seem so empty I just took in poor, vagabond
Huckleberry Finn, and I'd about made up my mind
to legally adopt him, when laws-a-me, he ran away
last week and I haven't set eyes upon him since. *(As
she speaks* BECKY *re-enters from* HARPER *house.
Taking* BECKY *by the hand)* So this was your first
day at our school?

BECKY. Yes'm—— *(As she speaks* WALTER POT-
TER *enters at* R.U. *He is a young man, resolute and
rather stern of aspect. He carries a large leather-
covered book in his hand.)* My! There's Teacher
now.

MRS. DOUGLAS. *(To* MRS. THATCHER*)* I reckon
you haven't forgotten Walter Potter.

WALTER. *(To* MRS. THATCHER*)* I used to be the
worst boy in your Bible Class.

MRS. THATCHER. *(Shaking hands)* And the
smartest!

MRS. HARPER. *(To* WALTER*)* Was my Joe at
school today?

WALTER. If he was I didn't see him. I reckon

Joe was studying his geography with Tom Sawyer and Huck Finn along the river.

MRS. HARPER. Playing hooky again! Well, I got to 'tend to him. Something's got into that child's head and I can't make out what it is.

MRS. DOUGLAS. *(To* WALTER*)* You going in to see Doctor Robinson?

MRS. HARPER. *(Looking off* R.U.*)* There's Doctor coming up the street with Mary Rogers now.

MRS. DOUGLAS. *(Moving off)* I'll tell him to hurry.

WALTER. *(Turning away)* Not on my account. I only want to leave this book and get another. *(Exit* WALTER *into office down* L.I. MRS. DOUGLAS *looks after him.)*

MRS. DOUGLAS. *(To* MRS. THATCHER*)* Walter's studying medicine with Doctor Robinson, and teaching school till he gets his diploma. *(To* BECKY*)* You run on, child—— *(Then as* BECKY *exits* R.U.*)* Did you notice how Walter looked when you said Doctor Robinson was coming up the street with Mary Rogers? Ain't it too bad about his father? *(To* MRS. THATCHER*)* You recollect him, old Muff Potter? Walter's made his own way—you might say —right up from the gutter. Of course Muff wasn't always so, but after Mrs. Potter died he took to drink and went right down to nothing. Well, goodby, and bring your sister soon. *(Exit* MRS. DOUGLAS R.U.*)*

MRS. THATCHER. *(Looking after* MRS. DOUGLAS*)* She don't change a particle, does she? I reckon Mr. Douglas left her pretty well off?

MRS. HARPER. Oh, my, yes! She's real rich. And that good-hearted. If Huckleberry Finn had stayed with her he'd never 'a' had to worry in this world. *(Exit* MRS. HARPER *and* MRS. THATCHER *into* HARPER *house.)*

(As they exit Injun Joe *enters* L.I, *and is just mounting the* Doctor's *steps when the door is opened by* Walter, *who is coming out.* Injun Joe *is dark and evil-looking, poorly but not raggedly dressed.)*

Injun Joe. *(Pausing at foot of steps as he sees* Walter*)* How are you, Walt? Is Doc Robinson inside there?

Walter. No, he isn't in.

Injun Joe. I'll come around again. *(He turns away.)*

Walter. *(Closing the door and following him down to* L.I*)* Joe, hold on! I want to talk to you a minute.

Injun Joe. *(Moving on)* Well, I can't stop now.

Walter. *(Following him)* I reckon you've got time to hear me——

Injun Joe. *(Pausing as* Walter *confronts him)* Depends on what you want to say. School teacher! Bah! I can remember the time you couldn't read nor write, like me.

Walter. *(In a low voice as he looks down the street)* Hold on, I tell you. It's about my father. You've been giving him whiskey for the last week— keeping him drunk. I don't know what you're doing it for—but if you do it again I'll take the law into my own hands and I'll horsewhip you as Robinson had you horsewhipped for stealing.

Injun Joe. You! Horsewhip me? You! You think it's safe, do you? Well, it ain't, not for you, nor for him. *(He threatens* Walter*)* I can remember the time I could 'a' wrung your neck with a twist of my fingers, and dropped you into the river.

Walter. I've warned you. Now get out of my way. *(As* Walter *speaks* Mary Rogers *enters with* Dr. Robinson, R.U.*)*

Mary. Walter!

DR. ROBINSON. How are you, Walt? Evening, Joe. Goodby, Miss Mary. See you tonight at choir practise?

WALTER. (To DOCTOR) I've been in to change a book.

DR. ROBINSON. Got what you wanted?

WALTER. Yes. (Shows book) Professor Grey's Anatomy. I saw some calls for you on the slate.

DR. ROBINSON. I'll take a look at them. (Exits into office L.I.)

(As DR. ROBINSON exits INJUN JOE crosses down to the window L.I, where, out of sight of MARY and WALTER, who stand at the HARPER gate, he taps on the DOCTOR'S window. The DOCTOR rolls up the shade, looks out, and makes a sign to INJUN JOE to wait, and then disappears from the window. INJUN JOE loiters off and exits L.I.)

MARY. (To WALTER as she stands at the gate) What were you saying to that man?

WALTER. Father's been drinking again.

MARY. Drinking with Injun Joe?

WALTER. Yes. He's always with him.

MARY. (Leaning over the gate) Promise me, Walter, you won't get into any trouble with that man. You know what people say of him—he's so revengeful.

WALTER. I'd like to break his neck for him.

MARY. You will be careful—promise me—for my sake, Walter!

WALTER. Whatever you say, Mary. But don't you worry about me. (Exit WALTER L.U.)

MARY. (Looking after him) Poor Walter! (Exits into HARPER house.)

(As MARY exits DR. ROBINSON comes to the door

of office, looks up and down the street, goes back into his office, runs up the shade of the window, runs up the window, and, sitting on the sill, leans out, looking up and down the street that crosses from L.1 *to* R.1. INJUN JOE *loiters on at* L.1 *and up to the* DOCTOR *as he sits on the window-sill.)*

DR. ROBINSON. Been having words with Walter Potter, eh?

INJUN JOE. He'd better look out what he says to me. I got a long score to settle with him, one of these days.

DR. ROBINSON. How's his father today, thirsty?

INJUN JOE. Dry as a bone.

DR. ROBINSON. You'd better let him have what he wants——

INJUN JOE. All right, if you say so.

DR. ROBINSON. Here's a couple of dollars—— *(Hands him bills.)*

INJUN JOE. *(Taking the money)* This ain't enough—I want more—I want five dollars.

DR. ROBINSON. Look here, Joe. You might as well know right now, you can't bleed me.

INJUN JOE. Bleed you? If you want your dirty work done, you've got to pay.

DR. ROBINSON. Dirty work!

INJUN JOE. Bah! I know what you're up to. You think Walt's got a chance with Mary Rogers and you want me to keep his father drunk, and disgrace him, so she'll throw Walt over. All right, but you've got to pay. *(Holding out bills)* This ain't enough—no, nor five ain't enough. You'd better make it ten or—I'll talk.

DR. ROBINSON. Talk, eh? Well, that's all you'll get from me, and mind you, keep a close tongue in your head or I'll have you horsewhipped for a slanderer, as I had you horsewhipped once for a thief.

INJUN JOE. Horsewhipped! That's what *he* threatened. I won't take it. By God, do you think I've forgot? It ain't safe for you to remind me of the cut of that whip.

DR. ROBINSON. Not safe, eh?

INJUN JOE. No, not safe!

DR. ROBINSON. Well, I'm going to speak to Sheriff Jones about you. You can't blackmail me. Who'd take your word against mine? Don't let me see you hanging around my place again, or I'll have you lodged in jail. I'm done with you. *(As he speaks he rises from the window, closes it, and pulls down the office shade.)*

INJUN JOE. *(Stands staring at the blank window)* Done with me, are you? No, I reckon you ain't, not yet—not you. *(Looking at the blank window.)* Nor him! *(Looking the way WALTER has gone, then exits L.I.)*

(As INJUN JOE exits AUNT POLLY comes to her door at R., steps to the gate, stops, pushes her glasses back upon her forehead and looks up and down the street. She is a middle-aged woman with a sharp but kindly visage.)

AUNT POLLY. *(Calling)* Tom! Tom! *(She looks down the street)* What's gone with that boy, I wonder? *(She calls again)* You, Tom! Well, I lay, if I get hold of you I'll—— *(Lifting her voice)* You, Tom——

MRS. HARPER. *(Enters from her house L. and leans over the fence, calling across to AUNT POLLY)* Your Tom come home yet?

AUNT POLLY. Yes, Tom slipped in at the back door not more'n a minute ago. He's been playing hooky again, going in a swimming with Huckleberry Finn. He gets more trifling every day—— *(She calls)* Tom Sawyer!

MRS. HARPER. (Calling) Joe! Joe Harper—Joseph Harper! Not a sign, and company here, and no kindlings cut!

AUNT POLLY. Tom! You, Tom! I ain't doin' my duty, Sereny. I'm a-laying up suffering and sorrow for that boy. Every time I let him off my conscience hurts me so, and every time I hit him a lick my old heart 'most breaks. He hates work more than he hates anything else, so I'd laid out to make him whitewash this fence, but I reckon he's cut and run. You, Tom!

SID. (Coming to R. door) Tom's coming right away, Auntie. He's mixing the whitewash back of the shed.

AUNT POLLY. You tell him to hurry right up or I'll skin him. I got to put my bonnet on and go over to sit with Mrs. Hoss Williams. She's so poorly since the burying this morning.

MRS. HARPER. (Looking off R.U.) My, there's that child again. Seems to me I never see her without she's got a teacup in her hand.

(Enter GRACIE MILLER, R.U.; a shrewish little girl with neglected hair and shabby dress. She carries a teacup in her hand.)

GRACIE. (Advancing) Please, Mis' Harper, my Ma wanted to know if you'd lend her the loan of a teacupful of butter, and two spoons. We got visitors to our house.

MRS. HARPER. Come inside, and I'll see if I can spare it. (Aside to AUNT POLLY) Visitors, and not enough vittles to put into their own mouths. (Exit AUNT POLLY into house R. MRS. HARPER and GRACIE exit into HARPER house.)

(As they exit DR. ROBINSON comes out of his office, locks the door and exits L.U. TOM SAWYER en-

ters from the house at R. *In his hand he car-*
ries a pail of whitewash and a brush. He is
barefoot and one toe is tied up in a white rag.
He comes out of the gate, puts down the bucket,
surveys the fence, makes a pass or two with the
brush. Pauses to survey the effect. Repeats the
operation, sighs deeply and sits down on a stone,
discouraged. SID *enters from the house,* R.,
carrying a pail and whistling "Buffalo Gals."
As TOM *sees him he brightens.)*

TOM. Say, Siddy, I'll fetch the water if you'll
whitewash some.

SID. *(Pausing)* Can't, Tom. Aunt Polly told me
I got to get the water and not stop fooling with
anybody.

TOM. Oh, never you mind what she said, Siddy.
Give me the bucket—she won't ever know——

SID. Oh, I dasn't, Tom!

TOM. I'll give you a marble! I'll give you a white
alley, a white alley, Sid! *(He holds alley out to*
SID.)

SID. I'd like to, Tom, but Aunt Polly's just set
on your doing it all.

TOM. And besides, if you will, I'll show you my
sore toe——

SID. *(Weakening)* Well, mebby—lemme see.
(Puts down the bucket, leans over as TOM *unwinds*
the wrappings from his toe.)

AUNT POLLY. *(Enters from the house. She wears*
her best black bonnet and carries her sewing-bag.
Seeing them, she advances silently and whacks SID
over the head with her handbag) Go along with you,
Sid—— *(Exit* SID *with pail* R.1. *To* TOM*)* Now,
sir! *(She taps his head with her thimble.)*

TOM. I wa'n't doing nothing, Aunt. Don't **you**
whack me.

(As TOM *speaks* GRACIE *comes from the* HARPER *house and exits* R.U. *with her teacup and spoons, a napkin over the top of the teacup.* MARY ROGERS *and* MRS. THATCHER *come to the* HARPER *gate.)*

AUNT POLLY. Umf! Well, you didn't get a lick amiss. I reckon you been into some other audacious mischief, like enough.

TOM. I don't reckon I can do much, Auntie, but I'll try. I ain't real well.

AUNT POLLY. Rubbage—what's the matter with you?

TOM. I don't reckon I ought to stand up much with my sore toe.

AUNT POLLY. Sore fiddlesticks! Go 'long about your work and see you don't play hooky until it's finished. When I come back from Mis' Williams, maybe I'll give you a dose of pain-killer, and learn you your Bible verses. *(Moving up)* You going my way, Mary Rogers? *(Exit* MARY *and* AUNT POLLY L.U. MRS. THATCHER *returns to the* HARPER *house.)*

TOM. Bible verses. Shucks. *(Working on the fence)* Dern it all! I never did see such ornery luck. Dern this old fence, anyway. I wisht it'd fall down an' rot. *(As* TOM *returns to his whitewashing,* BEN ROGERS *enters* L.I. BEN *is a boy of about* TOM'S *size, barefoot. He is eating an apple and impersonating a steamboat as he enters.* TOM, *aside, as he works)* Derned if it ain't Ben Rogers. Well, I won't take none of his lip.

BEN. *(Impersonating the steamboat, his arm making great circles for the paddle-wheels)* Stop her. Ting-a-ling! *(He slackens speed; takes the middle of the street; leans far over to one side as he draws up to the sidewalk.* TOM *works on quietly, paying no attention.* BEN *stares at* TOM*)* Ship up to back! Ting-a-ling-ling! *(His arms straighten at his side)*

Set her back on the starboard. Ting-a-ling-ling!
Chow-ch-chow-w-w-chow! *(His right hand describing stately circles for the wheel.* TOM *goes on whitewashing the fence, paying no attention until* BEN *bumps into him)*

BEN. Confound it! Can't you get out of the way,
Tom Sawyer? Don't you know I'm the "Big Missouri," and I'm a-drawing nine feet of water?

TOM. *(Looks at his work carefully; sweeps his brush along the board; looks at the result)* Why,
it's you, Ben. I wasn't noticing——

BEN. You're up a stump, ain't you? Played hooky
and now you got to work. I'm going in a-swimming,
I am. Don't you wish you could? Course you'd
druther work—wouldn't you? Course you would.

TOM. *(Looks at* BEN; *takes another sweep with the brush)* What do you call work?

BEN. Why, ain't that work?

TOM. *(Carelessly, as he goes on with the whitewashing)* Well, maybe it is, and maybe it ain't. All
I know is it suits Tom Sawyer.

BEN. Oh, come on, now. You don't mean to let
on you like it?

TOM. *(Whitewashing with his back to* BEN*)* Like
it? Well, I don't see why I oughtn't to like it. Does
a boy get a chance to whitewash a fence every day?
*(He steps back to note the effect of his last stroke;
adds a touch here and there; turns his head to one
side to criticise the effect.)*

BEN. *(After a pause)* Say, Tom, let me whitewash
some?

TOM. You? *(He pauses; considers)* No, no, I
reckon it wouldn't hardly do, Ben. You see, Aunt
Polly's awful particular about this fence—right here
on the street. If it was the back fence, I wouldn't
mind, and she wouldn't; but this fence's got to be
done very careful. I reckon there ain't one boy in

a thousand, maybe not in two thousand, that can do it the way it's got to be done.

BEN. No! Is that so? Come on—lemme just try, only just a little——— Say, I'd let you if you was me, Tom———

TOM. Ben, I'd like to, honest Injun, but there's Aunt Polly. Well, Sid wanted to do it the worst way, and she wouldn't let Sid. You see how I'm fixed. If you was to tackle this fence and anything was to happen to it———

BEN. Oh, shucks! I'll be just as careful—now lemme try——— Say, I'll give you the core of my apple.

TOM. Well——— *(Hesitating)* No, Ben, no. I couldn't. I'd be afeard.

BEN. I'll give you all of it.

TOM. Well, here——— *(Giving BEN the brush)* I reckon it's taking chances, but seeing it's you, Ben—

(As TOM eats the apple and BEN begins to work on the fence, HUCKLEBERRY FINN enters L.U., playing a lively tune on a jewsharp. He is a boy of about TOM's size and age, but ragged and unkempt. His coat trails behind him almost to the ground, his long trousers are rolled up and fastened by one suspender, his hat is a ruin and he is barefoot. In his hand he carries a dead cat suspended by its tail.)

TOM. Hello, Huckleberry.

HUCKLEBERRY. Hello yourself, and see how you like it.

TOM. What's that you got?

HUCKLEBERRY. Dead cat.

TOM. Lemme see him. My, he's pretty stiff. Where'd you get him?

HUCKLEBERRY. Bought him off'n a boy.

Tom. What did you give?

Huckleberry. I give a bladder I got at the slaughter-house.

Tom. Say! What is dead cats good for, Huck?

Huckleberry. Good for? Cure warts with——

Tom. No? Is that so? I know something that's better.

Huckleberry. I bet you don't. What is it?

Tom. Why, spunk water——

Huckleberry. Spunk water! I wouldn't give a dern for spunk water!

Tom. You wouldn't, wouldn't you? D'you ever try it?

Huckleberry. No, I hain't, but Bob Tanner did——

Tom. Who told you so?

Huckleberry. Why, Bob told Jeff Thatcher, and Jeff told Johnnie Miller, and Johnnie told Jim Hollis, and Jim told Ben Rogers——

Ben. *(From the fence)* Yep, he did.

Huckleberry. And Ben told a nigger, and the nigger told me. There, now!

Tom. How did Bob Tanner do it, Huck?

Huckleberry. Why, he took and dipped his hand in a rotten stump where the rain water was——

Tom. In the daytime?

Huckleberry. I'll 'low he did——

Tom. With his face to the stump?

Huckleberry. Yes, I reckon so.

Tom. Did he say anything?

Huckleberry. I don't reckon he did. I don't know.

Tom. Talk about trying to cure warts with spunk water, such a blame fool way as that! Why, that ain't a-going to do any good. You got to go all by yourself to the middle of the woods, where you know there's a spunk water stump, and just as it's

midnight, you back up against the stump and jam
your hand in and say: *(He chants the verse)*

"Barley corn, barley corn,
Injun-meal, shorts,
Spunk water, spunk water,
Swaller these warts."

And then walk away quick, eleven steps—*(Walks
backward)* —with your eyes shut, and turn round
three times—*(Turns round)* —and walk home without speaking to anybody, because if you speak the
charm's busted.

HUCKLEBERRY. Well, that ain't the way Bob Tanner done.

TOM. No, sir, you can bet it ain't, 'cause he's the
wartiest boy in this town, and he wouldn't have a
wart on him if he knowed how to work spunk water.
Say, Hucky, how do you cure 'em with dead cats?

HUCKLEBERRY. Why, you take your cat and go
and get in the graveyard 'long about midnight, when
somebody that was wicked has been buried; and
when it's midnight a devil will come—or maybe two
or three, and when they're taking that feller away
you heave your cat after 'em and say, "Devil follow
corpse, cat follow devil, warts follow cat. I'm done
with ye!" That'll fetch any wart.

TOM. Sounds right. When you going to try that
cat?

HUCKLEBERRY. Tonight. I reckon they'll come
after old Hoss Williams 'bout midnight.

TOM. That's so. Lemme go with you?

HUCKLEBERRY. Of course, if you ain't afeard.

TOM. Afeard! 'Tain't likely. Will you come
round and meow?

HUCKLEBERRY. Yes, I'll meow, and you meow
back if you get a chance. Last time you kept me
a-meowing around till old Harper went to throwing
rocks at me and says: "Dern that cat!" And so I
hove a brick through his window, but don't you tell!

(As HUCKLEBERRY *speaks,* MUFF POTTER *enters* L.1
with JOE HARPER. MUFF'S *dress is careless and
neglected, his appearance that of the village
drunkard. About fifty years old. In his hand he
carries a kite, a short fishing-pole is over his
shoulder and a cob pipe in his mouth.* JOE HAR-
PER *is about* TOM'S *age; has a bladder with a
string attached in his hand. As they enter* SID
enters R.1 *with the pail of water.)*

SID. *(Looks at* TOM *and* BEN*)* I 'low I'll tell
Aunt Polly on Tom Sawyer—— *(Exit* SID *into
house* R.*)*

JOE. Say, Muff, you recollect, when I gave you
that bag of tobacco I hooked off'n Father, you said
you'd make me a kite some of these days.

MUFF. My, you oughtn't to 'a' hooked that tobacco. I won't give you no kite for no such orney
thieving. No, I won't. You let go that kite. Ain't
I give you that bladder already?

JOE. *(Taking kite as* MUFF'S *hold relaxes)* My,
ain't she a dandy? *(Seeing* BEN *at the fence)* Say,
what's Ben Rogers sweating over that fence for?

TOM. Ben and me's the only boys that can whitewash that fence like it's got to be done.

JOE. Shucks! I bet I can.

TOM. I bet you can't.

JOE. I'll show you mighty quick.

TOM. Couldn't, Joe. It's that particular, I was
afraid to trust even Ben. Wasn't I, Ben?

BEN. I had to beg the awfullest way.

JOE. Say, is that so? Say, I'll lend you my kite
if you'll let me try.

TOM. I'd like to, Joe, but I can't. Ben ain't done
yet.

BEN. You wouldn't trust him, would you, **Tom**?

JOE. I could do it careful-like, just like Ben.

TOM. Do you reckon you could? Real careful?

Joe. Lemme show you. Say, I'll give you my yaller tickets for the school merit medal—and my kite.

Tom. Lemme see the tickets. Reckon Teacher'd know 'em? Well—*(Taking kite)* —you watch Ben and study how he does it, and when he's tired I'll let you try a little.

Joe. Oh, say, now, lemme try now. Lemme try and I'll give you all my tickets and my bladder.

Tom. I don't think much of that bladder.

Joe. It come out of old Hay's sow, didn't it, Muff?

Muff. I reckon that was her personal bladder. *(As he sits in the shade)* Any of you boys seen my son Walt since school let out?

Huckleberry. I seen him. He said he wanted to know if I'd saw you.

Muff. How'd Walt look?

Huckleberry. Looked as if he'd like to lick me.

Muff. Laws-a-mercy! *(Heaving a sigh)* I can't seem to satisfy Walt no ways. Here I went and reformed at eleven-thirty o'clock, this very morning, and was a-going to take the pledge at the temperance lecture at eight o'clock tonight. Lecturer promised me fifty cents if I'd come up an' take the pledge, and I didn't feel I ought to refuse it, and now I don't dare go home to get my other clothes for fear of the way Walt'll carry on. I been sleeping at the slaughter-house the last three nights, and I ain't fit to be seen. It's scandalous, ain't it?

Huckleberry. You couldn't hire me to take no pledge.

Muff. *(Looking at* Huckleberry*)* Seems to me, Huckleberry, you made a big mistake to quit the Widder Douglas the way you done. Ain't you ever going back to Cardiff Hill?

Huckleberry. Me go back to Cardiff Hill! No, siree! I've tried it, and it don't work. I can't stand them ways, nor them blamed clothes the widder got me. They don't seem to no air git through 'em, somehow, and they're so rotten nice I couldn't set down, nor roll round anywheres; an' I got to go to church an' sweat an' sweat. I hate them ornery sermons.

Tom. Well, everybody does that, Huck.

Huckleberry. Then what do they have 'em for? And my grub come too easy. I didn't take no interest in my vittles. And dad fetch it, I got to ask to go a-fishing. I got to ask to go a-swimmin'. Derned if I hadn't got to ask to do everything. The Widder wouldn't let me smoke, and she wouldn't let me chaw. She wouldn't let me yell. She wouldn't let me gap, nor stretch, nor scratch. Being respectable ain't what it's cracked up to be. It's just worry and sweat, and a-wishing you was dead all the time.

Tom. Mebby if you'd 'a' tried it a little longer you'd 'a' come to like it.

Huckleberry. Like it! Yes, the way I'd like a hot stove if I was to set on it long enough! No, sir-ee, I won't live in them cussed smothery houses. I'm going to be just like old Muff.

Muff. Like me! Now, you looky here, Huck! You looky here. You 'n' Tom been mighty good to me, an' I don't forget it. You ain't ever mocked me —nor throwed me up to Walt. Often I says to myself, "I used to mend all the boys' kites and things, and show 'em where the good fishing-places was, an' befriend 'em, an' now they mock at me—when I ain't steady—and shame my boy, Walt. But Tom don't, and Huck don't." Don't you grow up to be like me. Don't you ever get drunk, then you won't ever get mocked at an' throwed up to people. What time did I say I'd swore off today?

Tom. Half-past eleven this morning.

Muff. Eleven-thirty—yes, that was when. I recollect it was afore noon. Sing'ler I didn't wait until I took the pledge tonight. *(He rises and goes to fence)* I ain't laid on no whitewash in years. Say, Joe, let me show you a little. I won't do more'n a board. I don't want no scandalmonger to say I was a-workin'. They'd say Walt wasn't a-supporting me. You watch out, Bennie. (MUFF, *with* BEN, *works slowly off* R.I, *leaving* TOM, HUCKLEBERRY *and* JOE HARPER *alone upon the scene.* HUCKLE-BERRY *takes out an old corncob pipe and filling it, begins to smoke.)*

TOM. Say, boys, when we're pirates I know where we'll have our den!

JOE. Where?

TOM. Why, on Jackson's Island. You know, Hucky. It's five miles down the river, and it's got a haunted house on it.

HUCKLEBERRY. Cause old Jackson got murdered there. It's the bulliest place in the world.

JOE. By Jings, it'll be gay being pirates. Oh, I guess not!

TOM. Talk lower, Joe. We don't want Muff and Ben to hear. Don't you let on to them or they'll tell and we'd be pursued and captured sure.

JOE. I'd just like to see 'em try to capture me.

HUCKLEBERRY. What'd you do?

JOE. Do? I'd die first, that's what I'd do, after I'm a pirate! I reckon they'll feel pretty bad when it's too late. Then they'll wish they hadn't treated us just like dogs.

TOM. I tried to do right and get along, but they wouldn't let me. I hope Siddy and Aunt Polly'll be happy when I'm gone, and never feel sorry cause they drove me out into the world to suffer and mebby die.

HUCKLEBERRY. When do you reckon we can start being pirates? I want to get quit of this here town. I'm always running into the Widder Douglas, an' having to dodge and feeling mean. When we going to have the initiation and get our names and learn the countersign?

TOM. We'll do it tomorrow after school. It'll be just the life for me. When you're a pirate—you don't have to get up mornings, or go to school, or wash, or any of that blamed foolishness. A pirate don't have to do anything but take ships and burn 'em, and kill everybody.

JOE. They don't kill the women, do they?

TOM. No, they're too noble.

JOE. And don't they wear the bulliest clothes—oh, no—all gold and silver and diamonds!

HUCKLEBERRY. Who?

JOE. Why, the pirates.

HUCKLEBERRY. *(Looking disconsolately at his clothes)* I reckon I ain't dressed fittin' for a pirate, but I ain't got none but these.

TOM. Oh, just you wait till vacation time comes and we get to robbing. Then we'll show you!

(As TOM *speaks* BEN *re-enters with* MUFF R.I. *They are splashed with whitewash.* BEN *carries the whitewash brush and bucket.)*

BEN. *(Advancing)* Well, she's finished! *(As he speaks* INJUN JOE *loiters on at* L.U.; *pauses as he sees* MUFF. TOM *and* JOE HARPER *carry the bucket into house,* R.)

INJUN JOE. Got a job at whitewashing, Muff?

MUFF. *(Indignantly)* Me work! How you talk. I ain't able. *(To* BEN*)* Hand me that fishpole, Bennie.

INJUN JOE. Come on down to the wharf and try your luck. I'll be there when the "Big Missouri" runs into the dock.

MUFF. No, sir-ee! I ain't going near no steam-

boat barrooms. No, I ain't. I've quit. Ain't I, boys?
I quit at eleven-thirty this forenoon.

BEN *and* HUCKLEBERRY. Yes, Muff's quit.

INJUN JOE. Nobody asked you to have a drink.

MUFF. It wouldn't 'a' done no good if they had.
Say, Joe, when'll that boat be in?

INJUN JOE. I reckon she'll be on time. You coming?

MUFF. No, I ain't. I've swore off. Yes, I have.
Say, Joe, you don't believe me—well, I'll just go
down to the dock to prove it to you. I'm a-going to
take the pledge at eight o'clock tonight. *(Exit* MUFF
and INJUN JOE R.I.*)*

(As they exit BECKY *re-enters with* ALFRED TEM-
PLE, R.U. ALFRED *is an offensive, citified boy.
He wears shoes, a natty hat and a necktie.)*

ALFRED. *(As they enter)* There's Ben Rogers
talking to Huckleberry Finn. Let's pretend we don't
see him.

BEN. *(Aside to* HUCKLEBERRY*)* There's that
derned new boy. Derned Saint Louis smarty. Seen
him at school today.

HUCKLEBERRY. Come on, let's light out of this.
Let's go down to the swimmin'-hole.

BEN. I'll get licked if I go. Well, who cares for
a licking, anyway? *(Exit* HUCKLEBERRY *and* BEN
R.I.*)*

ALFRED. *(At* HARPER *gate)* Well, goodbye, Becky.
Mebby I'll be over after supper, if you'll be out.

BECKY. I'll be out if Ma'll let me.

ALFRED. I'm coming back this way pretty soon.
(As he moves to exit R.U.*)* Say, ain't this a one-
horse town! Oh, no, I guess not. Say, you can
just rub the moss off its back. *(Exit* ALFRED R.U.
BECKY *hangs about the* HARPER *gate.* TOM *and* JOE
HARPER *re-enter* R. *from house.* BECKY *catches*

Tom's *eye.* Becky *looks away, and throws a pansy over the fence.* Tom *hesitates.)*

Tom. *(To* Joe Harper*)* I reckon mebby I'd better wait till Aunt Polly comes.

Joe. Darned if I'd wait. *(Exit* Joe Harper r.i.*)*

Tom. *(Edges over to the fence, pretending not to see the pansy; gets his foot upon it, picks it up with his toes, and hops off with it and hides it in his roundabout.* Becky *comes down to the gate.* Tom *cautiously approaches)* You're Joe Harper's cousin, 'ain't you?

Becky. Yes, me and Joe are cousins.

Tom. I seen you in church on Sunday.

Becky. I saw you.

Tom. Did you?

Becky. I was at school today.

Tom. Was you? I played hooky. That's why I wasn't there. What's your name?

Becky. Becky Thatcher. What's yours? Oh, I know. I heard the teacher ask. It's Thomas Sawyer.

Tom. That's the name they lick me by. I'm Tom when I'm good. Say, Becky, you call me Tom, will you? *(They leave the* Harper *gate and advance to the shed near the fence at* r.i. Tom *takes up the whitewash brush and begins to mark on the shed.)*

Becky. What are you marking on the shed?

Tom. *(Working with his back to the audience)* Oh, it ain't anything.

Becky. Yes, it is.

Tom. You'll tell.

Becky. No, deed and deed and double deed I won't.

Tom. You won't tell anybody, ever, as long as you live?

Becky. No, I won't ever tell anybody.

Tom. Oh, you don't want to see.

Becky. Now that you treat me so I will see! *(There is a little scuffle. She pushes* Tom *from be-*

fore the shed where the words "I love you" are seen printed large on the boards) Oh, you bad thing! *(She slaps* TOM's *hands.)*

TOM. Say, Becky, was you ever engaged?

BECKY. Engaged, what's that?

TOM. Why, engaged to be married.

BECKY. No, not as I know of.

TOM. Would you like to be?

BECKY. I reckon so. What's it like?

TOM. Like? Why, it ain't like anything. You only just tell a boy you won't ever have anybody but him, ever, ever, ever, and then you kiss, and that's all. Anybody can do it.

BECKY. Kiss! What do you kiss for?

TOM. Why, that is to—well—seems like they always do it.

BECKY. Everybody?

TOM. Everybody that's in love with each other. You seen what I printed on the shed?

BECKY. Yes. *(Hanging down her head.)*

TOM. What was it, Becky?

BECKY. I shan't tell you.

TOM. Shall I tell you?

BECKY. Yes, but some other time.

TOM. No, lemme tell you now.

BECKY. No, not now—tomorrow.

TOM. Oh, no, now. Please, Becky. I'll whisper it ever so easy. *(He puts his arm about her, his lips close to her ear)* I love you. Now you whisper it to me.

BECKY. No, I won't.

TOM. Come on, Becky. It ain't fair not to, after I done it.

BECKY. Mebby I will, if you turn your face away so you can't see. But you mustn't ever tell anybody, will you, Tom?

TOM. No, indeed, indeed, I won't. Now, Becky! Don't you be afraid.

BECKY. *(As* TOM *turns his face away)* I love you, Tom. *(She springs away and runs up and down the street, with* TOM *after her. Then she takes refuge in a corner of the fence down* R.I, *covering her face with her apron.* TOM *clasps her about the neck.)*

TOM. Now, Becky, it's all done but the kiss. And that ain't anything at all. Please, Becky, nobody's looking, and it's most dark. (BECKY *drops her apron.* TOM *kisses her. They both wipe their mouths with the backs of their hands.)* There, it's all over, Becky, and always after this you know you ain't never to love anybody but me, and you ain't never to marry anybody but me—never—never and forever. Will you?

BECKY. No, I'll never love anybody but you, Tom, and I'll never marry anybody but you, and you ain't ever to marry anybody but me, either.

TOM. Certainly, of course not; that's a part of it.

BECKY. It's so nice. I never heard of it before.

TOM. Oh, it's ever so gay. Why, when me and Amy Lawrence was engaged——

BECKY. Amy Lawrence! Oh, Tom—then I ain't the first you've ever been engaged to—— *(She begins to cry)* I ain't the first!

TOM. Oh, don't cry, Becky; I don't care for Amy Lawrence any more.

BECKY. Yes, you do, Tom. Yes, you do—you know you do. (TOM *tries to put his arm about her, but she pushes him away.)*

TOM. Becky, I—I don't care for anybody but you. Becky, Becky, won't you say something? *(He takes up* JOE HARPER'S *bladder from beside the fence, and holds it out to her. He falters)* Please, Becky, won't you take my bladder?

BECKY. *(Striking the bladder to the ground)* I hate you, hate you, hate you! I'll never speak to you again! *(Exits into* HARPER *gate.)*

TOM. *(Following to the gate)* Becky! Come back,

Becky. Please, Becky. *(He hears a DOOR SLAM)*
Well, blame it all, don't come back if you don't want
to. Shucks! I don't care!

(As TOM *speaks* ALFRED *enters* R.U. *and goes toward
the* HARPER *gate.* TOM *turns from the gate.
They meet. Pause, eyeing each other. The
scene has darkened a little to evening.* TOM
turns up his nose. The BOYS *begin to sidle
slowly round one another.)*

TOM. *(After a pause)* I can lick you.
ALFRED. I'd like to see you try it.
TOM. Well, I can do it.
ALFRED. No, you can't, either.
TOM. Yes, I can.
ALFRED. No, you can't.
TOM. I can.
ALFRED. You can't.
TOM. Can.
ALFRED. Can't.
TOM. *(After a pause)* What's your name?
ALFRED. 'Tisn't any of your business, maybe.
TOM. Well, I 'low I'll make it my business.
ALFRED. Well, why don't you?
TOM. Smarty! You think you're some! Oh, what
a hat!
ALFRED. I dare you to knock it off. Anybody
that'll take a dare'll suck eggs.
TOM. You're a liar.
ALFRED. You're another.
TOM. You're a fighting liar and you dasn't take
it up.
ALFRED. Aw—take a walk.
TOM. Say, if you give me much more of your
sass I'll take and bounce a rock off'n your head.
ALFRED. Oh, of course you will.
TOM. Well, I will. *(Then, after a pause in which*

they sidle round EACH OTHER, *shoulder to shoulder)* Get away from here.

ALFRED. Get away yourself.

TOM. I won't.

ALFRED. I won't either. *(They stand shoulder to shoulder, each pushing against the other, each with one foot out to brace himself.)*

TOM. You're a coward and a pup. I'll tell my big brother on you and he can thrash you with his little finger, and I'll make him do it, too.

ALFRED. What do I care for your big brother? I've got a brother that's bigger than he is—and what's more, he can throw him over that fence, too.

TOM. That's a lie.

ALFRED. Your saying so don't make it so.

TOM. *(Drawing a line in the dust with his big toe)* I dare you to step over that. If you do I'll lick you till you can't stand up!

ALFRED. *(Stepping over the line)* Now you said you'd do it, now let's see you do it.

TOM. Don't crowd me. You'd better look out.

ALFRED. Well, you said you'd do it.

TOM. By Jingo, for two cents I will do it.

ALFRED. *(Taking two coppers from his pocket, he holds them out to* TOM*)* There's your two cents!

TOM. *(Strikes the coppers from* ALFRED'S *hand. They grapple, struggle, roll over in the dust.* TOM *comes up on top. Pounding* ALFRED*)* Holler 'nuff! Holler 'nuff!

ALFRED. *(In a choking voice)* 'Nuff!

TOM. *(Rising)* Now, mebby that'll learn you. Better look out who you're fooling with next time.

ALFRED. *(Brushing the dust from his clothes and sniffling as he moves off, now and then pausing to look back at* TOM*)* Just you wait till the next time I catch you out.

TOM. Oh, go on home, and don't give me none of

your lip. (*As* TOM *turns away* ALFRED *picks up a stone and throws it at* TOM, *then exits* R.U. TOM, *turning*) Derned sneak! I 'low I'll lay for him! (*As he speaks* AUNT POLLY *enters* L.U. *Advancing to meet her*) Mayn't I go and play now, Aunt?

AUNT POLLY. How much of that fence have you whitewashed?

TOM. It's all done, Aunt!

AUNT POLLY. Tom, don't lie to me. I can't bear it.

TOM. Just you look and see.

AUNT POLLY. (*Advances to a point from which she can survey the line of fence off* R.I) Well, I never! There's no getting round it, you can work when you've a mind to. But it's powerful seldom you've a mind to, I'm bound to say.

SID. (*Who has come to the door* R.) Auntie, Tom never done a lick of that whitewashing. He got Ben Rogers and Joe Harper to do it. He just talked to Huckleberry Finn and he's been fighting with the minister's grandson. I seen him from the window.

AUNT POLLY. Fighting! You, Tom Sawyer!

TOM. No, I ain't, Aunt.

AUNT POLLY. Oh, Tom, Tom, how can you lie so? (*Sternly*) Forty times I've said if you didn't stop talking to Huckleberry Finn I'd skin you. (*To* SID) Hand me that switch from beside the door! (SID *hands* AUNT POLLY *the switch. It hovers in the air.*)

TOM. (*With sudden inspiration*) My! Look behind you, Aunt!

AUNT POLLY. (*Whirls round, catching her skirts out of danger.* TOM *exits into the house in pursuit of* SID, *who flies before him.* AUNT POLLY *stands, surprised, a moment, then breaks into a gentle laugh*) Hang the boy! Can't I never learn anything? He 'pears to know just how long he can torment me before I get my dander up, and he knows if he can make out to put me off for a minute it's all down again, and I can't hit him a lick.

TOM. *(Reappears at door R.)* I never said I done it all, Aunt.

AUNT POLLY. Don't you stir out of that door again this night, or I'll tan you. *(Exit* AUNT POLLY *into house R.* TOM *exits into the house. The TWILIGHT deepens to evening. LIGHTS appear in house R.)*

*(*MR. SPRAGUE *enters; goes to Church door; unlocks it; goes in. In a moment LIGHTS appear in the Church windows.* VILLAGERS *loiter on and pass up the street, or exit through the Church door* C. MRS. DOUGLAS *enters* R.U. MRS. THATCHER *and* JUDGE THATCHER *enter from the* HARPER *gate and cross to the Church.)*

MRS. DOUGLAS. Lovely evening, ain't it? Where's Mrs. Harper?

MRS. THATCHER. Sister said she'd try to run over after she got the dishes done.

MRS. DOUGLAS. *(To* MR. SPRAGUE, *who reappears at the Church door)* You remember Mrs. Thatcher used to sing in our choir. Oh, my, yes, she did, and Judge Thatcher, too.

JUDGE THATCHER. I reckon my singing days are over.

MRS. DOUGLAS. Well, you just got to join in tonight at choir practice. Wasn't the hymns too lovely at Hoss Williams' funeral, and wasn't Mr. Sprague's remarks upliftin'? There's Sheriff Jones. He sings bass. (SHERIFF JONES *enters from* L.U. *To* JONES) I thought mebby Mary Rogers would have come with you.

JONES. I saw Walter Potter at their gate. I reckon he'll bring Mary.

MRS. DOUGLAS. Well, let's go in. I s'pose I've got to take the organ. (*Exit* ALL *into the Church.*)

(*As they exit* DR. ROBINSON *enters* L.U., *goes to his office door, unlocks it, goes in, LIGHTS his lamp, turns it down low, comes out, locks the door and is just starting across to* R.U. *when* WALTER *and* MARY *enter* R.U. *together.*)

DR. ROBINSON. (*Pausing as he sees them*) I was just going for you, Mary. (*Looking at* WALTER) I didn't know you had other company.

WALTER. (*Pausing*) If I'm in anybody's way—

MARY. (*Interposing*) Why, Walter—I didn't promise the Doctor.

(*As* MARY *speaks* MUFF *enters* R.I. *He staggers as he enters.*)

MUFF. (*Advancing*) Say, Walt, is that you? Lemme speak to you, Walt.

WALTER. (*Going to him*) Father! You've been drinking again!

MUFF. Me? I ain't had a drop. I'm dry as hay. I'm just going home for my other clothes—and then I'm a-going to take the pledge. Lecturer promised me fifty cents and I didn't feel——

WALTER. Father! Haven't you any shame?

DR. ROBINSON. (*To* MARY) Looks as if Walter had his hands full.

MARY. Yes, we'd better go in. (*She turns to Church door; pauses.*)

WALTER. (*Sternly, and in a low voice*) You've been drinking again with Injun Joe! That's the truth, isn't it?

MUFF. I ain't had a drop since forenoon.

WALTER. Father!

MUFF. Well, I ain't—except I did take a taste
with Joe down on the "Big Missouri"——

WALTER. Damn him! I knew it! And I'd told
him to let you alone.

MUFF. *(Seeing* MARY *on the Church steps)* Say,
Walt, Mary's waiting for you. Kinda sweet on
Mary, ain't you?

WALTER. Don't. She'll hear you. You can drag
me down if you want to, but don't you ever speak
her name with mine again. That's over. She shan't
have the shame of you. Let her take Robinson.
What's the use of hoping or trying? God! What's
the use? *(He turns from* MUFF, *moving up.)*

MUFF. Where are you going, Walt?

WALTER. I'm going to find Injun Joe!

MARY. *(Advancing)* Walter!

WALTER. *(Pausing)* Well——

MARY. Aren't you coming with me?

WALTER. No, not tonight. I can't—I've got to see
some one.

MARY. You'll come back for me?

WALTER. Yes. If I can—— *(Exit* WALTER R.U.*)*

(Voices are heard SINGING in the Church. MRS.
    DOUGLAS *comes to the door of the Church with*
    MR. JONES.)

MRS. DOUGLAS. You coming, Mary? Ain't no one
to carry the air.

MARY. Yes, I'm coming. *(Going to* MUFF*)* Oh,
don't you see how hard you're making it for Walter?

MUFF. *(Looking off)* Gone home, ain't he?

MARY. Won't you try to do better? Won't you
try for Walter's sake?

MUFF. *(Looking after* WALTER*)* Children warn't
brought up to treat their elders so in my time. 'Deed
they warn't.

DR. ROBINSON. *(To* MARY*)* Come! He's too drunk to know what you're saying.

MUFF. Drunk! Who says I'm drunk? *(He turns to* DR. ROBINSON.*)*

DR. ROBINSON. I say you're drunk.

MUFF. *(Pushing* MARY *away)* I got to speak to him! He ain't got no right to call names. Here, Doc, lemme tell you something. I don't want you to go trying to take Walt's girl away from him. It ain't right.

DR. ROBINSON. *(Angrily)* Get out of my way, you drunken loafer! Get out of my way, or I'll——

MUFF. Hold on, there, Doc. I reckon you don't own this street! Don't you call no names. I ain't too old to make you wish you hadn't—and I can prove it, too.

DR. ROBINSON. Don't you threaten me, you miserable sot!

MARY. *(Drawing* DR. ROBINSON *away)* Come, he doesn't know what he is saying. Come, Doctor, come!

MRS. DOUGLAS. Mary's right! Come! Let him alone. *(Exit* MARY *and* DR. ROBINSON *into Church, followed by* MRS. DOUGLAS *and* MR. JONES. *As they exit* MUFF *totters to the door of the* DOCTOR's *office,* L., *and collapses upon the steps.)*

MUFF. *(Muttering to himself)* Drunken loafer, that's what he called me. Well, he's got to let Mary Rogers be. It ain't right that Walt should worry so and take it out on me—it ain't right. *(He finds a piece of heavy board by the steps)* Hefty, ain't it. I reckon it'll make good kite-sticks for Tom Sawyer's kite. *(He takes out his knife and begins to split the piece of wood.)*

(As MUFF *sits on the steps the sound of VOICES floats out from the Church.* MUFF *nods and works and nods.* MUFF *hums the air of the hymn from the Church.* JOE HARPER *steals on*

at R.1 *and sneaks up to the* HARPER *gate.* MRS. HARPER, *who has come to the gate, sees him.)*

MRS. HARPER. Now, sir; so you've come home at last. Well, I reckon your father will have a word to say to you before you go to bed this night. Playing hooky with Huck Finn and Tom Sawyer again! And company here—— Ain't you ashamed?

JOE. Well, I been sick.

MRS. HARPER. Where you been sick?

JOE. I been sick to my stomach.

MRS. HARPER. What made you sick to your stomach?

JOE. I studied my spelling-lesson so hard I reckon it must 'a' hurt me.

MRS. HARPER. Your spelling-lesson! You walk right straight into the house this minute. *(Exit* JOE HARPER *and* MRS. HARPER *into* HARPER *gate.)*

(The MOON has risen and now lights the scene. MUFF nods on steps. The sound of a CAT meowing heard off R.1 *and* HUCKLEBERRY FINN *is seen in the shadow by* R.1 *fence, the dead cat in his hand. The MOONLIGHT brightens.* HUCKLEBERRY *meows again.)*

MUFF. *(Stirring as he dozes on the steps)* Scat, you devil! Scat! *(He throws a stone across at* AUNT POLLY'S *fence.)*

TOM. *(Is seen to crawl from his window out along the roof of the wing. He meows cautiously, then drops from the roof to the shed, and from the shed to the ground)* That you, Hucky?

HUCKLEBERRY. Yes, thought mebby you wouldn't come.

TOM. Well, I'm here, ain't I? You got the cat?

HUCKLEBERRY. Yep, I got her.

TOM. Then let's be going.

HUCKLEBERRY. *(Hesitating)* We needn't be afraid of anything as far as the tannery, but it's ornery mean up the hill to the graveyard after that.

TOM. I know it is. Say, Hucky, do you believe the dead people'll like it for us to go there?

HUCKLEBERRY. I wisht I knowed. It's awful solemn, ain't it? Do you reckon old Hoss Williams'll hear us talking?

TOM. Course he will. Least his sperrit will.

HUCKLEBERRY. I wisht I'd said *Mister* Williams, but everybody called him Hoss.

TOM. Sh!

HUCKLEBERRY. What is it?

TOM. Somebody's coming. Better hide till they go by. Come on up! *(As he speaks they scramble up on the roof of the shed at R.I.)*

DR. ROBINSON. *(Re-enters from Church and crosses to his office. He stumbles upon MUFF, half asleep upon the steps)* Who's this?

MUFF. *(Rousing)* That you, Walt?

DR. ROBINSON. Oh, it's you, is it? Sleeping off your drunk on my steps! I don't want you loitering here. Move, now! Move, I tell you!

MUFF. *(Rising)* Say, Doc, hold on—wait a minute. There's something I wanted to say to you.

DR. ROBINSON. *(Unlocking his office door and pushing it open)* I haven't any time to waste with you! Take yourself off! *(He goes into his office; turns up the LIGHT. The shade is up and he is seen moving in the room.)*

MUFF. *(Following to the door of the office and looking in)* Say, Doc, I got to speak to you. It's about Mary Rogers and my boy.

DR. ROBINSON. *(Appearing in the door again)* What's that you say?

(As DR. ROBINSON speaks INJUN JOE enters R.I. He

*half advances as if to speak, then pauses,
stealthily watching* MUFF *and* DR. ROBINSON.*)*

MUFF. Injun Joe says you're trying to take Mary
Rogers away from Walt. He says you've been giving him money to do it.

DR. ROBINSON. It's a lie! Injun Joe'll take it
back or I'll have him horsewhipped and run out of
town.

MUFF. *(Threatening* ROBINSON*)* Here, now!
Don't you talk like that about my pard. I won't take
it off'n you.

DR. ROBINSON. Drop that knife. (MUFF *drops
knife.)* I'll have you both jailed in the morning.
You can't come round here threatening me! By God,
you can't! *(He strikes* MUFF.*)*

(As the DOCTOR *strikes* MUFF *they grapple and
struggle near the office door. As they struggle*
INJUN JOE *advances stealthily, picks up* MUFF'S
knife, and goes round and round the struggling
MEN. *Suddenly the* DOCTOR *wrenches free from*
MUFF, *catches up the heavy piece of wood, and
fells* MUFF *with it to the earth. As the* DOCTOR
strikes, INJUN JOE *springs upon him and drives
the knife, hilt deep, into his side.)*

DR. ROBINSON. *(Seeing* INJUN JOE *for the first
time)* Joe!

INJUN JOE. *(Pushing him backward into the
office)* You'll horsewhip me! You'll jail me! *(The*
DOCTOR *staggers through the door into the office.*
INJUN JOE *follows and is seen to stab him again in
the lighted office; then he bends above him as he
falls, rifles the body, rises, pulls down the office
shades, blows out the* LAMP, *and comes to the door.
Looking back through the office door)* Dead! That
score is settled. Damn him! *(Then he sees* MUFF,

and stooping down, thrusts the knife in MUFF'S *hand. Then he shakes* MUFF *roughly by the shoulder.)*   *(WARN Curtain.)*

MUFF. *(Recovering; as he rises the knife is clutched in his hand. He looks up; sees* INJUN JOE*)* Joe! What's happened? *(Looking at the knife in his hand)* Where's Doc Robinson?

INJUN JOE. *(Pointing into the office)* You've done for him, Pard.

MUFF. *(Drops the knife from his hand. It falls by the steps)* You don't mean——

INJUN JOE. He's dead——

MUFF. Dead!

INJUN JOE. Turn the key on it afore you go. Give you more time afore they're after you. Turn the key. (MUFF *locks the door with trembling hand.* INJUN JOE *pushes the key into* MUFF'S *pocket, then pushes him out along the street)* Go. Get quit of the town afore sun-up. Move now, and don't leave any tracks behind you. *(He pushes* MUFF *off* R.I; *looks back as the MOONLIGHT brightens and shines in his face)* Fool! I reckon I've done for them both.

(The end of the HYMN drifts out from the Church.)

CURTAIN

ACT TWO

SCENE: *The Village School.*

The scene shows the interior of the bare schoolroom. The teacher's desk is upon a platform R. Behind it upon the wall are the blackboards and maps. Two uncurtained windows, R.C. and L. back; at L. is the door. The bell-rope dangles down on L. wall.

Beyond the windows are seen the fence with its gate half off its hinges, and the street at the edge of the village. The seats for the GIRLS are nearest the teacher's desk; back of them are placed the seats for the BOYS.

At rise, WALTER is seen to pass along the street beyond the windows, and enter the gate. He opens the schoolroom door and enters. He carries the book he borrowed in Act I from DR. ROBINSON under his arm. He crosses to the desk and places the book upon the desk. Then rings the bell, hangs up his hat beside the door, takes off his coat, finds a broom in the corner and begins to brush out the schoolroom. As he does so MARY ROGERS is seen beyond the windows, passing along the street. She enters the gate, then advances to the open door L. and

41

pauses in it. WALTER *does not see her, as his back is turned to the door.*

MARY. *(After a moment's pause)* Walter, aren't you going to say good morning?

WALTER. *(Turning)* Why, Mary, how'd you get here?

MARY. *(Laughing)* By the gate. I was going down to the store for some sugar. We're putting up peaches today. *(She holds out her basket)* I saw the door was open, so I just came in to ask why you didn't come back to take me home from church last night?

WALTER. *(Turning from her and going on with his sweeping)* I reckon you didn't miss me much. Doctor Robinson was there.

MARY. Doctor Robinson! Walter, Doctor Robinson isn't anything to me. I just won't talk to you. *(She moves toward the door.)*

WALTER. *(Still without turning)* Goodbye.

MARY. *(Turning back)* Walter—— *(Going to him)* I won't quarrel with you—so you needn't try to make me. My! What a dust you're raising. Give me that broom. It isn't a man's work. The Judge and Mrs. Thatcher and Mrs. Harper and Mrs. Douglas are coming to visit the school today with Mrs. Sprague.

WALTER. Lord, I wish they'd stay at home.

MARY. Please let me sweep out for you.

WALTER. I'm paid to do it.

MARY. No, you're not. You're paid to teach. Give me the broom. Yes, you shall. *(She struggles with WALTER for the broom.)*

WALTER. *(As MARY clings to the broom)* You'd better let go—Mary—don't. *(He puts the broom behind him.)*

MARY. How mean you are! *(In her eagerness*

MARY *puts her arms about* WALTER, *reaching for the broom, her cheek touches his coat. In an instant he clasps her in his arms, kissing her fondly.)*

WALTER. Mary! Mary! Mary! It's your own fault. It's your own fault.

MARY. *(Struggling in his arms)* Walter! Let me go! Walter! You don't know what you're doing. Walter—you must not.

WALTER. *(Releasing* MARY *and crossing to the desk)* I—I didn't mean to do it—I'm sorry—but I couldn't help it! *(He stands with his back to her)* I didn't want things to end this way between us— but they'd got to end some way.

MARY. *(Moving toward him)* To end—Walter! I don't see why—Walter—— *(She touches his hand with hers)* I don't want things to end between us— ever.

WALTER. *(Turns to her; sees her near him; draws her to him)* Mary, are you sure of that—you wouldn't fool with me—would you—and then throw me over! If you say it, Mary, you mean it, don't you?

MARY. I mean it, Walter.

WALTER. Then you don't care more for Doctor Robinson than you do for me?

MARY. I only care for you, Walter.

WALTER. *(Kissing her)* It's going to make a big difference to us, isn't it? I know *one* thing, it's going to bring you a lot of care and trouble.

MARY. And happiness, too, if you love me.

WALTER. If I love you?

MARY. Do you, Walter?

WALTER. I can't remember the time when I didn't love you, or when I wasn't jealous of you, and afraid you'd love someone else. I don't want you to give me any promise, Mary. It wouldn't be right—I've got Father to think of, but I reckon there isn't anything I'm afraid of now.

(The CHILDREN are seen gathering at the gate and along the fence outside.)

MARY. Did your father come home last night?

WALTER. No, Father didn't come home.

MARY. He had words with Doctor Robinson after you left. It worried me. *(Looking back at WALTER)* My, I wish those children weren't there.

WALTER. *(Drawing her from the door)* They won't see.

MARY. Yes, they will.

WALTER. Well, let them. *(He kisses her. MARY passes out through the L. door. WALTER looks after her. She pauses, with the CHILDREN all about her in the gate; smiles back at him.)*

CHILDREN. *(Outside)* Goodbye, Miss Mary! Goodbye!

MARY. Goodbye! Goodbye! *(Exit MARY. As she exits WALTER pulls the bellrope. The BELL rings above. The CHILDREN start with a rush for the door.)*

GRACIE. *(Outside)* My, that's the second bell. You let go of me, Ben Rogers, or I'll be late.

VOICES. Here's Becky Thatcher! Hurry up, Becky, or you'll catch it!

(As they speak the CHILDREN enter the schoolroom. GRACIE, ALFRED, BEN, SID, AMY LAWRENCE, BECKY and others, all with their books and slates. The CHILDREN hang up their hats on pegs beside the door and then go to their seats. BECKY and AMY sit near each other. There is one vacant seat between them. WALTER takes his place in his chair on the platform, takes up the large yellow calf-covered volume from his desk, and opens it, and then, his chin upon his hand, sits looking off through the window the

way MARY *has gone. There is a hum of voices
as the* CHILDREN *settle themselves.)*

(JOE HARPER *opens the door* L., *enters, hangs up
his hat and sneaks into his seat.)*

GRACIE. *(Aside to* AMY*)* My! Looky, there's
Joe Harper. I thought he'd run off again.

JOE. *(Aside to* BEN*)* If Teacher hadn't been
reading his old book, I reckon I'd 'a' caught it.

BEN. *(Aside to* JOE*)* What made you late?

JOE. Waited for Tom Sawyer. Ketch me doing
it again. How's the spelling-lesson?

BEN. Mighty dern mean. Some of 'em just cracks
my jaws. Can't seem to twist my tongue around
'em.

(WALTER *raises his eyes from his book and looks
over the school. Instantly there is silence. All
the* CHILDREN *bend their heads over their books.
Presently* WALTER *resumes his reading.)*

GRACIE. *(Aside)* Say, Amy, lend me the loan of
a slate pencil, will you? I broke mine yesterday.
Ma'll get me a new one next week, maybe.

AMY. *(Passing* GRACIE *a pencil)* It ain't very
sharp. I just can't learn this page, and if I miss it
I won't get the yellow tickets. Alfred Temple got
two yesterday, and he's sure to get the merit medal
before me.

GRACIE. Ben Rogers traded all his tickets for the
merit medal to Tom Sawyer. I reckon Tom'd trade
'em to you for a bag of peanuts.

AMY. My! That'd be cheating.

GRACIE. Not if you didn't get caught.

WALTER. *(Looking over the school)* Have any of
you boys seen Thomas Sawyer this morning? Sid-
ney, why didn't your brother come with you?

SID. I reckon Tom's going to play hooky again.

(As SID *speaks the door* L. *is cautiously opened.* ALL *eyes are turned upon it. There is an awful silence.* TOM SAWYER *enters, hangs his hat on a peg by the door, and attempts to sneak into his seat by* JOE HARPER.)

WALTER. *(Sternly)* Thomas Sawyer?

TOM. *(Pausing)* Sir!

WALTER. Come up here! *(Then as* TOM *advances)* Now, sir, why are you late again? And why were you absent yesterday, without excuse?

TOM. Me and Joe Harper felt sick.

WALTER. Sick, eh? Were you sick before school!?

TOM. No—well—my toe did bother me some, but we was sicker afterwards. Aunt Polly give me a dose of pain-killer, didn't she, Sid? I'll leave it to Sid if she didn't.

WALTER. Is that the best excuse you can give?

TOM. Well—say—lemme think a minute.

WALTER. You go and sit with the girls, and let this be a warning to you. No remarks, sir.

(A titter ripples through the room. TOM *hangs his head, goes to his desk for his slate and book, moves toward the* GIRLS' *side, and slips into the vacant seat between* BECKY *and* AMY. BECKY *tosses her head and hitches away from* TOM. *The* CHILDREN *nudge each other and wink.* TOM *appears to bend all his attention upon his book.)*

TOM. *(Aside to* BECKY*)* I just done it to sit by you, Becky. I don't care if I do get a licking. (BECKY *turns her head away.* TOM *pushes a peach over before* BECKY. BECKY *pushes it away.* TOM

puts it before her again) Please take it, Becky.
Come off of old Sprague's tree. I got more.

BECKY. *(Pushing the peach away)* I'd thank you
to keep yourself to yourself, Mr. Thomas Sawyer.
I'll never speak to you again.

TOM. Who cares, Miss Smarty? (TOM *hitches
over nearer to* AMY. *Presently he begins to draw
on his slate, hiding his work with his arm.)*

JOE. *(Holding up his hand)* Teacher!

WALTER. Well?

JOE. Please, may I pass the water?

WALTER. Yes, if anybody's thirsty. *(He con-
tinues his reading.* JOE HARPER *rises, goes forward,
takes up the bucket near platform and tin dipper
and passes the water.)*

BEN. *(As the water is passed to him)* Here,
gimme another dipperful!

JOE. My, you must think you're a cistern. You've
had three already. You'll bust yourself if you don't
watch out.

GRACIE. *(As it is passed to her)* My! I wouldn't
touch it. I seen a toad in the well yesterday.

(JOE HARPER *puts back the bucket and returns to his
    seat.* TOM *continues to draw on his slate.*
    BECKY *pretends not to notice.* AMY *becomes
    interested.* TOM *works on.* AMY *tries to see
    what he is drawing.* BECKY *becomes uneasy;
    eyes* TOM *furtively.* TOM *still ignores her.)*

AMY. *(Aside to* TOM*)* Let me see it.

TOM. There! *(He partly uncovers the slate)* It's
a house.

AMY. It's nice. Make a man.

TOM. *(Drawing)* There, that's a man.

AMY. It's a beautiful man. Now make me coming along.

Tom. *(Deftly spitting on his slate and rubbing it with his sleeve)* Wait a minute—— There—that's you.

Becky. *(Aside, but so that* Tom *can hear)* Some people think they're mighty smart, always showing off.

Amy. *(Looking at* Tom's *drawing)* It's ever so nice. I wish I could draw!

Tom. It's easy. I'll learn you! Ain't anybody I'd as lief teach as I would you, Amy. *(Watching the effect of his words on* Becky.)

(Walter *silently advances upon the unconscious* Pair. *He now lifts* Tom *by the ear and deposits him in his own seat, beside* Joe Harper. *There is an awful pause, during which* Walter *stands above* Tom. *Then he moves away to his seat.)*

Walter. Thomas Sawyer will be kept in during recess for whispering in school. The first class in spelling will now recite.

(Tom, Joe Harper, Ben, Alfred, Becky, Amy *and* Gracie *go up, and stand in a row before* Walter's *desk.)*

Walter. *(Opening the spelling-book)* Now, children—because?
Ben. *(Spells)* B-e-c-u-z——
Walter. Wrong! Thomas?
Tom. B-e-k-u-z——
Walter. Wrong. Alfred?
Alfred. B-e-c-a-u-s-e. *(Aside)* My, that's easy.
Walter. Beware.
Joe. *(Spelling)* B-e—be—w-a-i-r-e—waire——
Walter. Wrong. Rebecca?

BECKY. *(Nervously)* Be-w-a-y-r-i-e——

WALTER. Try again. Don't be afraid, Rebecca.

BECKY. *(Wildly)* B-e—be—w-a—way—i-r-e——

WALTER. Wrong. Amy?

AMY. B-e—be—w-a—wa—r-e—re!

WALTER. Right. Now, Gracie. Before?

GRACIE. B-e—be—f-o-u-r-e—for.

WALTER. Wrong. Benjamin?

BEN. B-e—be—f-o-w-r-e—for——

WALTER. Wrong. Thomas?

TOM. B-e—be—— *(To* ALFRED*)* You stop a-punching me—or I'll——

WALTER. Thomas Sawyer!

TOM. Well, he was a-crowding me.

WALTER. Before?

TOM. Be——be—f-o-w-r-u-e——

WALTER. Wrong. Alfred?

ALFRED. B-e-f-o-r-e.

WALTER. Right.

TOM. *(Aside to* JOE*)* I'll lick the stuffings out o' him yet. Just see if I don't.

WALTER. *(To* JOE*)* Despise?

JOE. *(Desperately)* D-e-s—des—p-y-s-e——

WALTER. Wrong.

JOE. Dern it all. Seemed to me it was that way.

WALTER. Rebecca—— Now don't be frightened.

BECKY. D-e-s—des—p-i-s-e—pise.

WALTER. Right.

BECKY. Oh, my! Ain't I glad!

WALTER. Now, Amy, desperate.

AMY. D-e-s—des—p-e-r—per—r-e-i-g-h-t—rate.

WALTER. Wrong. Gracie, see if you can't do a little better.

GRACIE. D-e-s—p-e-r—per—r-a-k-i-t-e.

WALTER. I didn't ask you to spell kite.

GRACIE. *(Aside)* What's he a-picking on me for?

WALTER. Benjamin. Desperate?

BEN. D-e-s—des—p-u-r-r-a-t-e.

WALTER. Wrong. Thomas. Desperate?

TOM. D-e-s—des—p-a-i-r—per—r-e-u-i—— I mean y—right.

WALTER. Go to your seat, sir, and learn your lesson! You're a disgrace to this class! *(As WALTER speaks door L. is timidly opened and MUFF looks in, half entering. His face is wan and frightened.)*

MUFF. Walt! Say, Walt!

WALTER. *(Looking up)* Father—— *(He pauses)* Well?

MUFF. Say, Walt, can I see you outside a minute?

WALTER. *(Looking at the CHILDREN before him)* I'm sorry, Father. I'm busy now hearing a class. You go home, and I'll see you at noon.

MUFF. Just a minute, Walt! Please, Walt!

WALTER. Can't now, Father. I'll be home at noon.

MUFF. *(Turning away)* It's all right, Walt. It's all right. I oughtn't to 'a' come. I'll be going now. It's all right. Goodbye, goodbye. *(Exit MUFF L. As he exits he stumbles on the steps. The CHILDREN titter.)*

WALTER. *(Fiercely)* Don't laugh at him. *(He follows to the door)* Father! Wait—what is it you wanted? *(He opens door; looks down the road)* Father! *(He reaches for his hat as if to follow MUFF. As he does so MRS. DOUGLAS, MRS. THATCHER, JUDGE THATCHER, AUNT POLLY, and MRS. HARPER, followed by MR. SPRAGUE, enter the gate and approach the door.)*

CHILDREN. My! See the visitors!

WALTER. *(Hanging up his hat as he sees them)* No use.

AMY. *(Aside to BECKY)* My, looky! There's your Ma with Mrs. Douglas and the Minister.

BECKY. That's my Pa, too.

WALTER. *(To* CHILDREN*)* The first class in spelling is dismissed!

(MRS. DOUGLAS, MRS. THATCHER, MR. SPRAGUE, JUDGE THATCHER, AUNT POLLY *and* MRS. HARPER *enter* L.*)*

AUNT POLLY. *(Advancing as the* CHILDREN *go to their seats)* Good morning, Walter. Good morning, children. Mrs. Harper and I thought we'd bring the Judge and Mrs. Thatcher over to see our school, and see how their Becky's getting along.

WALTER. *(Placing chairs)* Please take chairs on the platform?

MR. SPRAGUE. *(Aside to* WALTER*)* I trust you have not given out the merit medal for last week?

WALTER. Not yet.

MR. SPRAGUE. How fortunate! It will be a memorable occasion to our young friends if Judge Thatcher presents it.

MRS. DOUGLAS. *(Taking up* WALTER'S *book)* Still studying your doctor's book?

WALTER. Still studying. That's the book I borrowed from Doctor Robinson yesterday.

AUNT POLLY. I just stopped at Doctor Robinson's house as we come by to tell him to go in to see Mrs. Hoss Williams. She's so poorly.

TOM. *(Rising in his seat, pale and excited)* Say! Had Doctor Robinson come home yet?

AUNT POLLY. *(Staring at* TOM*)* No. His sister said he must 'a' been called out late last evening, and hadn't got back. Office locked up and the shades pulled down

MRS. DOUGLAS. *(Laughing)* Anybody sick at your house, Tom?

TOM. *(Collapsing into his seat)* No'm—I—I thought I'd show him my sore toe—it's mortifying

AUNT POLLY. *(Laughing)* His sore toe! Drat the boy, he does look sick.

MR. SPRAGUE. *(Standing on platform)* Children, this is Judge Thatcher, who has come all the way from Constantinople, in Union County, to see you, and to present the merit medal to the boy or girl who has received the most merit marks during the past week. (TOM *takes tickets for which he had traded in Act I from his pocket, and begins to count them.*) Now, children, I want you all to sit up just as straight and pretty as you can, and give me your attention.

BEN. *(Aside)* My, ain't old Sprague spreading himself?

MR. SPRAGUE. *(Looking over the* CHILDREN*)* If there is any little boy here with twelve yellow tickets, he can come up right now and receive his reward of merit medal, and shake hands with our visitors. (TOM *rises and goes forward.* SPRAGUE, *aghast*) You, Thomas!

TOM. *(Handing up tickets)* Nine yaller tickets, ten red tickets and six blue ones; makes twelve yeller tickets.

MR. SPRAGUE. The possession of these tickets is conclusive evidence—*(Hesitates, then turns to* JUDGE THATCHER*)* —that Thomas Sawyer has received one hundred merit marks during the past week.

AUNT POLLY. *(Aside to* MRS. HARPER*)* Laws a-mercy! For playing hooky, I presume.

BEN. *(Aside)* What dern fools we was to trade Tom those tickets.

JOE. Might 'a' knowed what to expect.

JUDGE. *(To* TOM*)* Ah—a fine little man! What is your name, my boy?

TOM. *(Apparently tongue-tied)* Tom——

JUDGE. Oh, no—not Tom! It is——

Tom. *(With difficulty)* Thomas.

Judge. Ah, that's it. I thought there was more to it, maybe. But you have another, I daresay.

Mr. Sprague. Tell the gentleman your other name, Thomas, and say, sir.

Tom. Thomas Sawyer—sir!

Judge. That's it. That's a good boy. Fine, manly little fellow. A hundred merit marks in one week. That's a great many, and you never can be sorry for the trouble you took to earn them, for knowledge is worth more than anything there is in this world. It's what makes great men and good men. You'll be a great man and a good man yourself some day, Thomas, and then you'll look back and say it's all owing to the precious school privileges of your boyhood days. It's all owing to your dear Teacher, that taught you to learn, and the dear Superintendent who encouraged you and watched over you, and gave you this beautiful medal. That is what you will say, Thomas, and you wouldn't take any money for those hundred merit marks—no, indeed, you wouldn't. And now you wouldn't mind telling me some of the things you've learned in school? No, I know you wouldn't, for we are proud of little boys that learn. Now, no doubt you know the names of all the Twelve Disciples. Won't you tell us the names of the first two who were appointed?

Mr. Sprague. Answer the gentleman, Thomas. Don't be afraid.

Mrs. Thatcher. *(As Tom hangs back)* I know you'll tell me. The names of the first two Disciples were——

Tom. David and Goliath!

Walter. *(Ringing the bell)* Recess!

Children. Recess! Recess!

Aunt Polly. Recess! My, it's a mercy!

MRS. DOUGLAS. Well, I feel better about Huck's leaving me. I reckon it ain't so easy to bring up a boy. *(The CHILDREN rise, take their hats from the pegs and exit.)*

MRS. THATCHER. Come with us, Becky.

MRS. DOUGLAS. You going our way, Walter?

WALTER. Yes, Mrs. Douglas. *(To TOM)* You, sir, see that you don't leave this room till school takes up again.

MRS. DOUGLAS. *(Aside to WALTER)* David and Goliath!

TOM. *(Aside to JOE HARPER)* If you see Huckleberry Finn hanging round the alley, ask him to come over to the window. (JOE HARPER *nods. Exit L. ALL but* TOM. BECKY, *half hanging back, looks at* TOM, *then exits with her mother.* TOM, *looking after* BECKY) Maybe now she'll want to make up. Well —let her! *(He goes to* R.C. *window)* Hello, Hucky. Come on over. Ain't nobody here.

HUCK. *(Appearing at window* R.C.*)* Being kept in, ain't you?

TOM. Teacher's got a spite at me. Come on inside!

HUCK. I reckon it ain't safe.

TOM. Oh, yes, it is. Nobody'll be back for half an hour.

HUCK. *(Climbing in through the window)* My! Ain't it an ornery place! Clean as a church, and 'most as mean looking! And you got to sit in here and sweat every day? What's them there? *(Pointing to maps.)*

TOM. Them? Oh, that's maps of North America and Europe—'most all the world!

HUCK. What they for?

TOM. To show where places is.

HUCK. Sounds unlikely. *(Taking up* WALTER'S *book from the desk)* What's this?

TOM. My, don't you drop that! That's a doctor's

book. Teacher's gone and forgot to lock it up. Lemme see it! (TOM *takes the book from* HUCK *and examines it. Spelling it out*) Professor Grey's An-a-tomy—Anna Tommy.

HUCK. What's that?

TOM. Mebby it's a woman's name.

HUCK. Say it again.

TOM. Anna Tommy.

HUCK. That's it. Anna Tommy! It's about some woman. Let's see inside. Looky there, Tom.

TOM. *(As they look at the pictures)* Why, some of 'em ain't got a stitch on! Nice kind of doctor's book. I should think he'd better keep it locked up. Teacher borrowed it off Doc Robinson yesterday.

HUCK. Doctor Robinson? Ain't heard any news yet, have you?

TOM. *(Placing the book on the desk)* No, only Aunt Polly said she'd stopped at his house, and he hadn't come home. I 'most keeled over!

HUCK. Them office blinds ain't moved. He must be inside there. Injun Joe done for him sure.

TOM. Huckleberry! What do you reckon'll come of this?

HUCK. If Doc Robinson's dead, I reckon hangin'll come of it.

TOM. Who'll tell? We?

HUCK. I been thinking about that. Suppose somethin' happened and Injun Joe didn't hang. Why, he'd kill us some time or other, just as dead certain as we're a-standing here. If anybody tells, let Muff Potter do it, if he's fool enough.

TOM. Mebby Muff Potter don't know it.

HUCK. What's the reason Muff Potter don't know it?

TOM. Because he'd just got that whack when Injun Joe done it. D'you reckon he could see anything?

HUCK. By hooky! That's so, Tom.

TOM. We better go and look if we can see into Doc Robinson's window when school lets out.

HUCK. My, Tom, we'll know soon enough. I expect to hear 'em hollering any minute. Keeps me all of a shiver.

TOM. Me too. *(After a pause)* I reckon we're safe as long as we keep mum.

HUCK. Looky here, Tom. Let's take and swear to one another—that's what we got to do—swear to keep mum.

TOM. Yes, swearing's the best thing. It's more surer.

HUCK. Would you just hold hands and swear that we——

TOM. Hold hands! No, sir! That won't do. There's got to be writing 'bout a thing like this— and blood!

HUCK. Blood! Yes, I reckon that's so.

TOM. Reach me that new shingle out of Benny Roger's desk. I got a piece of red keel. We can write it with that, and sign our initials in blood.

HUCK. *(Gets shingle and hands it to TOM)* Now you're talking. You write it, Tom.

TOM. *(Writing laboriously)* "Huck Finn and Tom Sawyer swears they will keep mum about this, an' they wish they may drop down dead in their tracks if they ever tell, and rot."

HUCK. My, Tom, that's strong.

TOM. I reckon it'll hold when we make our initials in blood. Got a pin? Gimme it.

HUCK. *(As TOM takes the pin and pricks his finger)* Don't it hurt?

TOM. *(Squeezing out a drop of blood)* Some, but I reckon we can't be too particular. *(He draws on the shingle)* T. S. That's for Tom Sawyer. *(Then to HUCK)* Hold out your hand.

HUCK. Ouch—don't you stick me.

TOM. Hold still. Don't holler. I ain't a-hurting you. (*Pricks* HUCK'S *finger. He marks with* HUCK'S *finger on the shingle*) H. F. That's for Huck Finn. (*Viewing his work*) I reckon that'll hold now.

HUCK. (*Suddenly, as the figure of* INJUN JOE *appears at* L. *door*) Oh, Jiminy! It's him!

TOM. (*Turning to door*) Injun Joe!

INJUN JOE. (*Pausing in the doorway*) Walt here?

TOM. No—no, he ain't.

INJUN JOE. Gone home, has he?

TOM. I—I reckon so.

INJUN JOE. I heard he was 'round town lookin' for me last night. Thought I'd stop in an' see what he wanted. (*He half turns away, then turns back*) Ain't seen anything of old Muff Potter, have you? He ain't been around, has he?

TOM. Muff was here, but he didn't stay.

INJUN JOE. Here, was he? Which way did he go when he left?

TOM. Down the road.

INJUN JOE. Toward town?

TOM. No, 'tother way.

INJUN JOE. What's that you got in your hand, Huck?

HUCK. Me? Nothing.

TOM. It's only a shingle we was a-marking on.

INJUN JOE. Lemme see. Huck learning to write? (*He takes the shingle from* HUCK *and turns it in his hands*) What's the matter with you boys? You act like you was afear'd of me. (*Looking at the shingle*) What you been writing here?

TOM. (*Aghast*) Bible verses. I was a-teaching Huck—(*He stammers*) —his cattikism.

(*VOICES of the* CHILDREN *returning are heard in the distance.* INJUN JOE *turns to the door.*)

INJUN JOE. If you see Muff Potter, you tell him I was a-lookin' for him. And you tell Walt. I reckon he'll see me soon enough. *(Exit* INJUN JOE. *The* BOYS *follow to the* L. *window, watching him go out at the gate and slouch off along the road.)*

TOM. If Injun Joe could 'a' read what was on that shingle, we'd 'a' been dead now.

HUCK. I reckon we'll be safer when that shingle's buried. We'll light out for Jackson's Island tonight, won't we, Tom?

TOM. There ain't nothing in this world can hinder me and you and Joe Harper being pirates now. Jackson's Island will see our gang afore morning.

HUCK. I'd better sneak. See you after school lets out. *(Exit* HUCK FINN *through the window* R.C.*)*

TOM. Hold on a minute, Hucky. We better fix about the countersign and I've got the bulliest names for all of us. You're to be Huck Finn, the Red Handed, and Joe Harper's—— *(His voice is lost as he disappears. He follows* HUCK *through the window.)*

(BECKY *enters with a bunch of flowers which she places on the teacher's desk. As she is turning away her eyes rest on the book* WALTER *has been studying. She takes it up, opens it, standing with her back to the door. As she turns the pages of the book* TOM *enters at the door* L. *and cautiously advances toward her.)*

TOM. *(Whose entrance is unobserved by* BECKY) Becky! Please make up, Becky, won't you?

BECKY. *(As she hears* TOM'S *voice she starts guiltily and the book falls to the floor. A page is torn out)* Tom Sawyer! You are just as mean as you can be to sneak up on a person and look at what they're looking at!

TOM. *(Indignantly)* How should I know you was looking at anything! (TOM *picks up the book, puts the torn page back, and lays the book on the desk)* My! You done it now.

BECKY. *(Beginning to cry)* Oh, what shall I do? What shall I do? *(Turning to* TOM*)* You know you're going to tell on me. I'll be whipped, and I never was whipped in school. *(She stamps her foot)* Be so mean if you want to! Hateful! Hateful! Hateful!

TOM. *(Half aloud for* BECKY'S *benefit)* Never been licked in school! Shucks! What's a licking? Well, it's a kind of a tight place for Becky Thatcher. All right, though. Let her sweat it out!

(The CHILDREN *enter* L., *laughing and talking, and take their places.* WALTER *enters, following them. He advances to his desk; pauses; turns to the* CHILDREN.*)*

WALTER. Did any of you boys see my father at noon?

JOE. No, I didn't.

BEN. I didn't, either.

GRACIE. I thought I seen him down in the alley, back of Doctor Robinson's office, but I ain't sure.

WALTER. *(Taking up the book from his desk)* I want one of you boys to leave this book at Doctor Robinson's for me after school.

BECKY. *(Aside)* Oh, he has it! *(Just as* WALTER *is about to close his book and turn to the* CLASS, *the torn leaf flutters out. He sees it.)*

WALTER. *(Turning to the* CHILDREN*)* How did this happen? *(To* TOM*)* Hand me that page. *(He takes it)* Torn out! Who tore this book? It is Doctor Robinson's book. It isn't mine. It's a borrowed book—a book I can't replace. I've told you

fifty times never to touch the books upon my desk.
Benjamin Rogers, did you do this?

BEN. No, sir.

WALTER. Joseph Harper, did you?

JOE. No, sir.

WALTER. Amy Lawrence?

AMY. No, sir.

WALTER. Gracie Miller?

GRACIE. No, sir.

WALTER. Are you sure?

GRACIE. Hope I may die if I did.

WALTER. Rebecca Thatcher, did you tear—no—
look me in the face—— Did you tear this book?

TOM. *(Springing forward before* BECKY *can
speak)* I done it.

VOICES. *(Heard in the distance)* Doctor Robinson's murdered! Go for the bloodhounds! Track
the murderer!

(MARY ROGERS, *white as a ghost, appears in the
doorway* L. *She leans for support against the
door.)*   *(WARN Curtain.)*

WALTER. *(Seeing her)*   Mary! *(Listening)*
What's that?

MARY. Walter—your father—oh, thank God he
isn't here!

WALTER. Father! What's happened?

MR. SPRAGUE. *(Appearing at the door with* JUDGE
THATCHER*)* They've found Doctor Robinson in his
office—murdered.

JUDGE THATCHER. They've found your father's
blood-stained knife beside the door.

VOICES. *(Off* R.*)* Doctor Robinson's murdered!
Doctor Robinson's murdered!

(VILLAGERS *are seen hurrying by along the street*

beyond the window R.C. HUCK FINN *appears
at the window* R.C., *where* TOM *joins him.*
CROWD *appears in door* L.)

WALTER. My father! Oh, my God! It's a lie!
Who accuses him? *(As he speaks* INJUN JOE *parts
the little crowd at the doorway and faces* WALTER.)
INJUN JOE. I do. School-teacher—I seen him do
it. (WALTER *moves angrily toward* INJUN JOE.
JUDGE THATCHER *and* MR. SPRAGUE *hold him back.)*
TOM. *(At window, aside to* HUCK) We've got to
tell.
HUCK. We can't. We've swore.

CURTAIN

ACT THREE

AUNT POLLY's *House.*

*The scene shows the interior of the living-room.
A door leads to the street at L.1. Up L. a bed
is placed, with valance to the floor. At R.1 is
an open fireplace with old andirons. At R.C. is
a door leading into the kitchen. There is an old
cupboard with blue dishes set against the wall
L. of R.C. door. A table in the Center of the
room. In the corners are cornucopias full of
dried grasses and berries. Wax flowers are on
a side table, under a glass case. A rag carpet
covers the floor, an old easy rocking-chair
stands by the table. A what-not is in R. Upper
corner.*

*The whole place is very neat and clean. On
the table lies an open Bible and a little heap of
TOM's clothes.*

It is TWILIGHT.

*There is a KNOCK upon the door L. AUNT
POLLY enters from the kitchen door R.C., pauses,
her hand upon her heart.*

AUNT POLLY. No—it can't be any news of Tom.
They wouldn't knock. They'd come right in. Likely
it's Mis' Harper to ask if I've heard anything.
(Opens door L.) Oh, it's you, Gracie. Will you
walk in, child?

GRACIE. *(As she enters L.)* My Ma sent me over to ask if you would please lend her the loan of two flatirons, and a cake of yeast? She's going to set bread tonight.

AUNT POLLY. You'll find them flatirons on the hearth in the kitchen. *(She crosses to the cupboard at R.)* You tell your Ma my yeast ain't very fresh, but I ain't had the heart for anything since Tom's been gone. *(She puts her apron to her eyes.)*

GRACIE. Oh, please, I want to hurry. They're a-going to send the old ferryboat down the river, with a cannon on it, and they're a-going to fire it off, just like they done last summer when Billy Turner got drowned. Maybe it'll bring Tom up, an' Joe, but Ma says she reckons Huck Finn's been so bad he'll sink right through to hell. Oh, please! I must hurry!

AUNT POLLY. You find it, Gracie. I can't see. *(Wiping her eyes with her apron.)*

GRACIE. *(Standing on a chair and looking into the cupboard)* I got it. *(Pausing aloft)* My, ain't them doughnuts grand.

AUNT POLLY. Come down, and I'll give you a fresh one. Ain't no one to eat 'em, these days. Sid don't care for 'em, and I can't touch 'em, now Tom's gone. But Tom, he'd hook a doughnut if my back was so much as turned for a second. I been frying some fresh ones. I thought if he did come home, the first thing he'd do would be to look in that cupboard for a doughnut. I didn't want to disappoint him.

GRACIE. My! *(At kitchen door)* I can smell 'em! *(Exit GRACIE into kitchen.)*

AUNT POLLY. *(Calling after her)* You bring me that cullender!

GRACIE. *(From kitchen)* I reckon Tom'd liked these, if he'd been alive! *(Re-enter GRACIE with the flatirons and carrying a colander, heaped with doughnuts.)*

AUNT POLLY. Put some in your pocket if you want to, Gracie.

GRACIE. Oh, may I? Me and Johnnie's so lonesome since Tom an' Joe Harper's got lost.

AUNT POLLY. You take some of them doughnuts home to Johnnie.

GRACIE. Not mine.

AUNT POLLY. No, take more. *(She places the colander on the cupboard shelf)* Can you carry the irons? I'll put the yeast in your apron.

GRACIE. *(As* AUNT POLLY *helps her with the irons)* My! Looky! Everybody's a-hurrying to the wharf!

AUNT POLLY. *(Looking through window)* I reckon they've got Muff Potter at last. Or maybe— my Tom—— *(As she speaks* MRS. THATCHER *and* MRS. DOUGLAS *come to the L. door and enter. Looking at their faces)* No? Still there ain't no news of Tom—and Joe?

MRS. DOUGLAS. Nor Huckleberry. No. No news. They're sending the old ferryboat out to search the river for the last time.

AUNT POLLY. I thought perhaps there'd be some word before night. They ain't found Muff Potter yet?

MRS. THATCHER. Not yet. But it ain't likely he'll escape with them Saint Louis detectives on his trail.

MRS. DOUGLAS. They say they're going to bring him back to town if they find him and lynch him in front of Doc Robinson's office.

AUNT POLLY. It's awful for Walter and Mary Rogers. People ought to think of them. *(A low BOOM is heard from the distance.)* Hark! What's that?

MRS. THATCHER. I wonder——

AUNT POLLY. It ain't thunder—becuz thunder—

MRS. DOUGLAS. Hark! Listen! It's on the river. *(She goes to window.)*

GRACIE. I know! It's the cannon on the ferry-boat. They're shooting it off to bring the boys up to the top. My! I want to see. *(Exit GRACIE L. The low BOOM is heard again. MRS. DOUGLAS and MRS. THATCHER turn to AUNT POLLY in sorrow.)*

AUNT POLLY. *(To MRS. DOUGLAS)* They've been gone since Tuesday night, and here it's Saturday.

MRS. DOUGLAS. *(To comfort AUNT POLLY)* It's all nonsense. Those boys've just run off, and Huck Finn along with them. Didn't they take Mr. Harper's boat? Didn't I see Joe Harper going along toward the water that very evening with a pair of oars? And now that they're searching both shores of the river, they'll find them. I wouldn't wonder any minute to see them walk right in at that very door.

AUNT POLLY. Wouldn't you? I've set up every night since Tom's been gone, in that chair there, and the lamp burning in the window—watching an' waiting for him to come home.

MRS. DOUGLAS. Well, you go to bed tonight. I reckon Tom's been sleeping sound enough. *(There is a KNOCK. AUNT POLLY rises and opens the L. door, revealing MARY ROGERS.)*

MARY. May I come in? I didn't want to go home. They don't see things as I do, and I'm all unstrung. *(She sees the OTHERS; pauses.)*

AUNT POLLY. You come right in, Mary. There —there—don't take on. It'll all be right in the Lord's good time. We all of us 'a' got our cross to bear.

MARY. *(Clinging to AUNT POLLY)* Oh! You don't know—you don't know. It isn't for me—and it isn't for Walter. It's for that poor old man. What'll he think of me—and what'll Walter think —speaking against him at the inquest?

AUNT POLLY. It ain't your fault, child. You couldn't help it. Others seen them words too. And Injun Joe told enough to hang ten men. But there's one comfort—they ain't got Muff Potter yet.

MARY. What Injun Joe said doesn't help me. It only makes it worse. It was so mean and cruel to throw the last straw, and to think of him hiding somewhere like a dumb animal, with every hand against him, and he Walter's father, Walter's own father——

AUNT POLLY. *(Signing to* MRS. DOUGLAS *and* MRS. THATCHER *to leave her alone with* MARY*)* There, don't you take it so to heart, child. Don't you take it so to heart.

MRS. THATCHER. My! Ain't it terrible when it's brought right home to you? *(Exit* MRS. DOUGLAS *and* MRS. THATCHER L.*)*

MARY. *(Raising her face from* AUNT POLLY'S *breast as they exit)* I know Walter hates me. I know he'll never care for me again, now that I've spoken against his father—— *(As she speaks there is a KNOCK on the door* L.*)* Somebody's at the door. I'll go into the kitchen and wait. I didn't want to worry you. I wanted to ask about Tom. (MARY *goes into the kitchen.* AUNT POLLY *opens* L. *door; sees* WALTER *standing there.)*

AUNT POLLY. Why, Walter! Won't you walk in and sit?

WALTER. *(Entering)* I wanted to ask if there's any news of the boys? I—I always though a lot of Tom. Father always thought a lot of Tom, too.

AUNT POLLY. An' Tom always thought a deal of you, Walter, and a deal of him. *(The cannon BOOMS in the distance.)* No, we ain't had no new word yet. They're firing a cannon over the water, and searching both shores of the river for some trace of the boys, or Lawyer Harper's boat, but they ain't found none yet. But no news is good news, I reckon. Leastwise, I pray it is. Maybe there'll be some word afore the day's done. *(She looks from window)* 'Most dark, ain't it? I hadn't noticed—— Well, maybe it'll come tonight. I ain't took off my clothes one night since they went away, just set there in my chair and dozed. I don't feel no need of sleep. Won't you set? *(Motioning him to a chair.)*

WALTER. Not tonight. I'd have liked to hunt for Tom, and Joe and Huck, if it hadn't been for Father. But you see, I want to be right here if they find him and bring him back. You know what they threaten—— They'll lynch him if they can. He hasn't got anyone but me.

AUNT POLLY. Yes, I reckon your place is here.

WALTER. Well, I'll be going.

AUNT POLLY. *(Hesitates, then speaks)* There's somebody that'd like to speak with you, Walter.

WALTER. *(Pauses; turns back)* Mary? Is she here?

AUNT POLLY. She just stepped into the kitchen when you knocked. Shall I call her?

WALTER. No. *(He turns to go)* Don't.

AUNT POLLY. You won't see her?

WALTER. I'd better not.

AUNT POLLY. *(Laying her hand on his arm)* I would, if I was you, Walter. She feels so bad about having to testify at the inquest. She thinks you hold it against her. I'll go fetch a light—and tell her who's here. *(Exit AUNT POLLY R.C. As she exits WALTER moves as if to call her back; pauses, irresolute, then moves as if to exit L. As he does so MARY enters from R.C. She pauses, seeing WALTER.)*

MARY. Walter—you're not going—without a word to me?

WALTER. *(Turning back)* What's there to say?

MARY. You've judged me, then. You've judged me for telling what I'd seen at the inquest.

WALTER. You couldn't help saying what you did. I know Father hasn't a better friend in the world than you, Mary.

MARY. Oh—Walter! Then can't we be friends?

WALTER. There's no hope of saving Father—and so there's no hope for you and me being happy together. It's all over between us, Mary. There isn't anything left for us but to say goodbye——

MARY. You don't love me, not as you did, Walter?

WALTER. No, not as I did.

MARY. Walter!

WALTER. I love you so much more now that I know I've got to give you up.

MARY. If you love me, it never shall be goodbye between us, Walter, never, never.

WALTER. It's got to be. When this hell is over I'm going away from this town.

MARY. I can go with you.

WALTER. No, you couldn't.

MARY. Yes, I could. I could.

WALTER. I wouldn't let you.

MARY. Walter! Why?

WALTER. *(Turning to her)* I'm afraid of myself. If it was in my father to kill, maybe it's in me! I tell you, I'm afraid to meet Injun Joe.

MARY. Injun Joe?

WALTER. I'm afraid of what'll happen.

MARY. Walter—you wouldn't—now——

WALTER. I don't know. I can hold out a little longer, but if they get Father—if they lynch him—as they threaten—and I know it was that man's doing! *(He turns to MARY)* I want to stand clear—I don't want to drag anyone down if I fall.

MARY. *(Clinging to him)* Walter—Walter! Don't

think of such things. We'll do our best. We'll do
right. We'll try always. And we'll win—Walter—
we'll win—we together—you and I—— Maybe
your father will escape them—maybe yet.

WALTER. *(His arms about her)* Not with that
price set on his life, and the whole town against
us. *(As he speaks* AUNT POLLY *enters* R.C., *bringing
a light. VOICES are heard off* L.*)*

MARY. *(At window)* It's Mrs. Harper.

AUNT POLLY. *(Advancing eagerly toward the
door, the light still in her hand)* Sereny! She
wouldn't come out unless there was some word about
them boys. *(The* L. *door is pushed open.* MRS. HAR-
PER *enters, followed by* MRS. DOUGLAS *and* SID.
AUNT POLLY *puts down the light with trembling
hand)* Sereny! Why don't you speak—— *(She
shakes her gently)* Sereny, I just can't endure no
more suspense—I reckon you're all a-weepin' for
joy? Where's Tom? Who found him? When's that
boy going to stop his nonsense and come home?

MRS. HARPER. *(Weeping)* Never. Never—we'll
never see our boys again in this world.

AUNT POLLY. Sereny! You don't mean—— No
—it ain't so. Mis' Douglas, my Tom—my boy!

MRS. DOUGLAS. *(Holding out* TOM'S *cap)* They
found Mr. Harper's boat upside down on the Missouri shore, five miles below—and Tom's cap—
caught on a snag of driftwood, a little further
down——

AUNT POLLY. *(Vaguely taking the cap and turning it in her hand)* It looks like Tom's—yes, it looks
like Tom's—— I put that button on with white
thread—— You remember, Siddy? *(She fondles
the cap in her hands, and sinks slowly and quietly
into her seat beside the table)* You don't reckon
there's any more hope, then, Sereny!

MARY. *(Aside to* WALTER*)* We'd better go.

WALTER. Isn't there anything to do?

MARY. Nothing tonight—tomorrow, maybe.

WALTER. Shan't we say something?

MARY. No, she isn't noticing. *(To* MRS. DOUG-LAS*)* I'll come over in the morning. *(Exit* MARY *and* WALTER, L. *As they go they leave the door a little open. It is unobserved.* ALL *are now seated about the table with their backs toward the door at* L.*)*

AUNT POLLY. *(Turning* TOM'S *cap in her hand)* My Tom, my boy, my boy! It don't seem as if I could understand it, Sereny. I reckon I didn't know how tired I was—or what a store I'd set on Tom's coming home. You don't reckon I'll ever see that boy again?

MRS. DOUGLAS. Not in this world of sorrow. Your Tom's right with the angels now.

AUNT POLLY. Oh, God forbid! *(As she speaks the door* L. *is cautiously and stealthily pushed open, and* TOM'S *bare head is seen peering into the room from the darkness.)*

TOM. *(Aside)* My! There's company! *(He crawls in cautiously and disappears under the bed.)*

MRS. DOUGLAS. What makes the light flare so?

SID. Why, the door's open!

MRS. DOUGLAS. Mary must have left it open when she went out with Walter. Go 'long and shut it, Sid. (SID *rises and closes the door* L. *just as* TOM *disappears under the bed.)*

SID. I don't reckon we'll ever see Tom come through that door again. (TOM'S *head appears under the valance of the bed.)*

AUNT POLLY. Oh, Mrs. Douglas, I don't know how to give him up. He was such a comfort to me, although he did torment my old heart out of me 'most; but he warn't bad, so to say, only mischiev-ous—only just giddy, and harum-scarum. He never meant any harm, and he was the best-hearted boy that ever was.

MRS. HARPER. It was just so with my Joe; always full of his devilment, and up to every sort of mischief; but he was just as unselfish and kind as he could be. And now I'll never see him again in this world—never—never—— *(She weeps bitterly.)*

MRS. DOUGLAS. *(Wiping her eyes)* Of course, Huckleberry wasn't kin to me—and he was real trying in some ways—but oh! I'd taken that boy right into my heart, and to think he's lying dead somewheres, poor, motherless thing, and no one to shed a tear for him! *(She weeps)* If he'd only come back to me! Oh, if I only hadn't tried to make a Christian of him. It was making him go to church that drove him away. Them long sermons—— They were long, you know they were, Sereny. No matter how instructing, they were almost more than a body could sit through. Huck might 'a' been alive now if them sermons hadn't been so long. I'll always hold it against Reverend Sprague. It's sinful, I know, but I'll hold it against him.

MRS. HARPER. Only last Sunday my Joe busted a firecracker right under my nose, and I sent him sprawling. Little did I know then how soon—— Oh, if it was to do over again—I'd hug him and bless him for it!

AUNT POLLY. I know—I know just how you feel. No longer ago than Sunday noon, my Tom took and filled old Peter, the cat, full of pain-killer, and I did think the cre'tur' would tear the house down and—God forgive me—I cracked his head with my thimble. Poor boy! Poor dead boy! (TOM *sniffles under the bed.)* But he's out of his troubles now, and the last words I ever heard him say was to reproach—— *(She breaks down utterly. TOM wipes his eyes, half crawls out as if to go to his aunt, then draws back hastily, as the door opens L. and* MRS. THATCHER *enters, with* BECKY, *followed by* MR. SPRAGUE.)

MRS. THATCHER. *(As she enters)* Step in, Mr. Sprague. Step in. *(To* MRS. HARPER) Sister, Mr. Sprague came to visit you in your hour of affliction, and I brought him right over.

AUNT POLLY. Siddy, let Mr. Sprague have your chair. *(To* MR. SPRAGUE) Oh, it's dreadful to bear, ain't it? *(Drawing* BECKY *to her)* If I only knew where that boy was tonight!

MR. SPRAGUE. Ah, Thomas is with his little comrade, Joseph, tonight, treading with light and joyous steps the green pathways of the bright tomorrow.

MRS. DOUGLAS. *(Weeping)* Where do you reckon Huckleberry is?

MR. SPRAGUE. Ah, Ma'am, we cannot look to see his erring feet treading the golden paths. We cannot expect to see his lost soul at the great reunion. From this sad picture we avert our eyes. Yet what a lesson—what a signpost on the path of life—these two virtuous youths led into evil courses and to tragic ends by bad example.

MRS. DOUGLAS. *(With indignation)* I don't care what you say. Huckleberry wasn't a bit worse than Tom Sawyer or Joe Harper. Not a bit—and he'd never had their advantages. I don't believe the Lord's going to forget that child never had any bringing up.

MR. SPRAGUE. I ask you, Mrs. Douglas, was Huckleberry Finn a professing Christian?

MRS. DOUGLAS. *(Angrily)* No, he wasn't! And he might 'a' been here now, alive and well, if I hadn't tried to make him one. He couldn't stand your sermons—that's what made him run away from my house—your long sermons. You ain't blameless about that boy. And if he isn't lost in hell this very minute, it's no thanks to you, Mr. Sprague.

MRS. THATCHER. Law—Mrs. Douglas, you don't know what you're saying.

MRS. DOUGLAS. Yes, I do. Yes, I do. It ain't right to pick on Huck, and I won't set still an' see it done.

SID. I hope Tom's better off where he is—but if he'd been different in some ways——

AUNT POLLY. *(Glaring at him)* Sid! Not a word against my Tom, now that he's gone! God'll take care of *him!* Never *you* trouble *your*self, sir!

MR. SPRAGUE. *(Collecting himself)* I mentioned to Mrs. Thatcher that it seemed fitting to have the funerals preached tomorrow.

AUNT POLLY. The funerals—— Oh, no, no, not yet!

MRS. THATCHER. There's no need to put it off.

MR. SPRAGUE. I have already spoken to Mr. Harper.

MRS. HARPER. I suppose it's best. *(To AUNT POLLY)* You ain't no objection?

AUNT POLLY. No. None as I think of.

MRS. THATCHER. *(To AUNT POLLY)* Is there anything you'd like Mr. Sprague to say?

AUNT POLLY. Not as I can think of now.

MR. SPRAGUE. Do you recall any of Thomas's favorite Scripture passages?

AUNT POLLY. Don't seem to me as I recall any —just now.

MR. SPRAGUE. Surely Thomas must have had some favorite hymns.

AUNT POLLY. Not as I recall—Tom warn't much on hymns.

MRS. THATCHER. Well, I should say "Rock of Ages"—and there's that lovely new tune, "In the Sweet Bye and Bye." If I ain't taking too much upon me—and Sister, there's your black clothes to fix.

MRS. HARPER. *(Rising)* Yes, I better go.

MRS. THATCHER. *(To* AUNT POLLY*)* Want I should send anyone to sit with you, tonight?

AUNT POLLY. No, I'd just as lief be alone, and Sid'll be here. Goodnight, Becky.

BECKY. *(To* AUNT POLLY*)* Goodnight, and oh— *(She whispers)* —when I say my prayers, I always ask the Lord to send Tom back again.

AUNT POLLY. That's right, dear, that's right. Mebby He'll hear ye, yet.

MRS. HARPER. Well, goodnight!

MR. SPRAGUE. Goodnight. Goodnight, Mrs. Douglas. *(He holds out his hand.)*

MRS. DOUGLAS. Goodnight, Mr. Sprague. *(Then as she takes his hand)* Mebby I was hasty.

MR. SPRAGUE. Not at all. Likely I was a-forgetting the good Lord's mercy. I reckon it goes a sight further than the longest sermon.

AUNT POLLY. *(To* MRS. HARPER, *with trembling lips)* Goodnight.

MRS. HARPER. *(Moves to* L. *door, then pauses and turns back to* AUNT POLLY, *throwing her arms about her)* Oh, ain't it hard?

AUNT POLLY. *(With a trembling voice)* I reckon we don't know how hard yet, Sereny! Not yet—not yet. *(She follows to the* L. *door. As the door is opened)* Wait, I'll fetch the light. *(She takes the light from the table and holds it in the open doorway as* MRS. HARPER *and* MRS. THATCHER *exit* L.*)* Can you see to get across the street?

MRS. THATCHER. Yes, we can see. You going to put on mourning for Tom?

AUNT POLLY. Such as I have.

MRS. THATCHER. We'll call when we get across the street. *(Exit* MRS. DOUGLAS, MR. SPRAGUE, MRS. THATCHER, BECKY, *and* MRS. HARPER. AUNT POLLY *stands in the doorway, holding the light aloft to shine out on the street.* MRS. THATCHER, *heard outside)* We're across. Goodnight.

AUNT POLLY. Goodnight. *(She pauses a moment, then closes the door; returns the lamp to the table; sees* SID*)* I reckon you'd better go upstairs to bed now, Siddy. You put your shoes out and I'll black 'em for you, and brush your other clothes for church.

SID. *(Lighting a candle at the lamp)* I'll have time to do that in the morning, Auntie. You'd better go to bed, too.

AUNT POLLY. I don't reckon I'll sleep much tonight. It don't seem right to go to bed, an' Tom not here. Go on upstairs, child—and, Sid——

SID. *(Pausing)* Yes, Auntie?

AUNT POLLY. I reckon you better kiss me goodnight.

SID. *(Kissing her)* Goodnight, Auntie.

AUNT POLLY. Goodnight. *(Then as* SID *is at the door* R.C.*)* You won't forget your prayers, Siddy, or to pray for your brother Tom, will you?

SID. No, Auntie. *(Exit* SID, *sniffling,* R.C. *As he exits* AUNT POLLY *goes to the old bureau* R., *opens it, and with trembling hands takes out her best bonnet and unfolds an old crepe veil; goes to table and begins to fasten the veil upon the bonnet. As she works she wipes her eyes quietly. Presently she puts by the things, and kneeling down by the bed, prays softly.)*   *(WARN Curtain.)*

AUNT POLLY. I—I'm only an old woman, and I know I'm unworthy of God's mercy. I—I won't ask much, but if you've taken my boy from me, Lord, don't hold his little faults against him. Lay 'em all to my charge, a lone old woman, who never had the heart to punish him—my own dead sister's boy. Blame me, not him, for his heart was always good. But I reckon that He who said "Suffer the little children to come unto" Him'll watch over my Tom.

(There is a pause during which AUNT POLLY *bows her head and prays silently)* Amen! *(She rises from her knees, goes to the table, takes up the lamp, places it in the window, and turns it down a little)* I'll let it burn for Tom tonight, where he'll see it shining if he does come home, and maybe the good Lord'll let him see it even if he ain't to ever come. I reckon I ain't too tired to watch this one night more. *(She sits in the rocking-chair beside the table; takes the great Bible in her lap, holding* TOM's *cap lovingly in her hand. Slowly as she turns the leaves of the Bible she nods and sleeps, her hands still fondly clutching* TOM's *cap. She moans a little in her sleep)* My boy—my Tom—my Tom—— *(As she sleeps* TOM *crawls cautiously from beneath the bed, takes a large piece of sycamore bark from his pocket, and steals toward the table.)*

TOM. *(Reading from the bark)* "We ain't dead. We're only off being pirates." *(He places the bark upon the table at her side, then steals to the cupboard, opens it, finds the doughnuts and begins to stuff his pockets with them. Looking at* AUNT POLLY*)* I reckon that bark'll ease her mind. *(He moves from the cupboard; pauses)* No. She'd tell— and then there wouldn't be any funeral! My, that'd spoil it all! *(He goes to the table, takes up the piece of bark, puts it in his pocket; then turning away, he moves toward the* L. *door, raises the latch and opens the door; looks back at* AUNT POLLY *sleeping in her chair; hesitates, then tiptoes back to* AUNT POLLY, *kisses her softly as she sleeps, picks up his cap from her lap, steals to the door, pulls on his cap and slips out into the night, leaving* AUNT POLLY *asleep in her chair by the table.)*

CURTAIN

ACT FOUR

SCENE I

The Pirate's Camp on Jackson's Island.

The Scene shows a half overgrown forest glade which many years before had been a partial clearing. At L.1 are the ruins of the old haunted house. In the thick forest growth at R. a sail is drawn over a fallen tree, R.C., forming a rude shelter. Near this a low camp fire smoulders out. Back of the camp the forest trees shut in the scene. Vines hang from the branches, and festoon from tree to tree. Through the trees and vines and undergrowth the gleam of the great river is seen.

At rise MOONLIGHT floods the scene, throwing into relief the haunted house, and throwing dense patches of shadow about it. The camp is in shadow. The smouldering embers of the camp fire are reflected in a dull glow upon the sail spread over the fallen tree to make a shelter. An OWL is heard hooting in the distance. An answering hoot comes from the further distance.

JOE HARPER. *(His voice coming from within the improvised shelter, R.C.)* Say, Tom—say, Hucky, didn't you hear something moving over there by the haunted house?

77

HUCK. *(Crawling to the door of the shelter)*
Only a possum in the bushes, I reckon.

JOE. Where's Tom? He ain't under his blanket.
He ain't here. Hucky, Tom's gone.

HUCK. Oh, no, I reckon not. *(Calling softly)*
Tom! Tom Sawyer!

JOE. He's gone an' left us, that's what he's done.
Nice kind of pirate he is.

HUCK. *(Louder)* Tom! Oh, Tom!

JOE. *(In a whisper)* Don't holler so, Huck, or
you'll fetch the ghost out of the ha'nted house. Old
Jackson's buried right 'round here somewheres.

HUCK. Pap said he remembered hearing about it
when he was a boy. Pap said Murrell's gang used
to rob up and down both sides of the river, and one
night, 'bout midnight, they got to fighting among
themselves and old man Jackson got killed right
there in that house. No one ain't ever lived there
since.

JOE. My, Hucky, don't talk about it. Supposin'
Tom don't come back?

HUCK. Tom ain't gone far. He's around somewheres on the watch.

JOE. I bet he ain't. I bet he's gone home, an' I
reckon he's gone to stay.

HUCK. Well, if that's so I'd never a-though it of
Tom Sawyer to run away in the middle of the night
and desert the gang.

JOE. Let's go down to the shore and see if he's
there.

HUCK. *(Examining his hat)* Why, looky here,
Joe. Here's something in my hat. It's a writing on
a piece of sycamore bark.

JOE. *(Taking it)* Le's see. It's Tom's writing.

HUCK. You read it, Joe. I'll poke up the fire.

JOE. *(Reading by the light of the camp fire)* "If
I ain't back afore sun-up, you'll know that Tom

Sawyer, the Black Avenger of the Spanish Main, is drowned."

HUCK. He says he'll be back afore sun-up.

TOM. *(Appearing at* L.U. *and pausing in the light of the camp fire)* Which he is.

JOE. Who goes there?

TOM. *(Advancing, a ham in one hand and his pockets bulging)* Tom Sawyer, the Black Avenger of the Spanish Main. Name your names.

JOE. Joe Harper, the Terror of the Seas.

HUCK. Huck Finn, the Red Handed.

TOM. 'Tis well. Give the countersign.

ALL. Blood!

TOM. *(Throwing down the ham)* There's something for breakfast.

HUCK. Where you bin?

JOE. What made you go?

TOM. Why, when you both went to sleep and I was sitting on the log on watch, I got to thinking we just ought to know the lay of the land round town afore we started in to rob much; see if anyone suspicioned us, or was going to send out to capture us.

JOE. My, they'd better not try that, not after the way they treated us and drove us away just like dogs.

HUCK. Better not fool around trying to capture me.

TOM. Well, when you was both asleep I wrote on the bark and put it in Huck's hat, and then I swam across the bar and got back to town as the bell was a-striking nine. I sneaked along behind a high board fence where a lot of loafers was talking on 'tother side 'bout Muff Potter and a thousand-dollar reward that'd been offered for his capture, an' how they was a-going to lynch him right afore Doc Robinson's office if they ever laid hands on him. When I got to Aunt Polly's house the door wasn't shut tight, so I crawled in and got under the bed in the sitting room, and no one seen me do it.

JOE. My, s'pose they'd a-captured you!

HUCK. What'd you a-done, Tom?

TOM. Done! I'd a-died in my tracks first, that's what I'd a-done.

HUCK. What you see after you got in?

TOM. Why, there set Aunt Polly an' Mis' Harper, an' the Widder Douglas an' Sid, all talking 'bout us. I could hear every word. My, boys, they've found the boat we came down to the island on—an' they think we've all been drowned—— Ain't it splendid?

JOE. My, it's gay!

HUCK. It's nuts, ain't it?

TOM. I hooked some doughnuts out of the pantry. They got wet some when I swam across the bar. Have one—— *(As they eat)* Say, what would the boys say if they could see us now?

JOE. Say, they'd just die to be here. Hey, Hucky?

HUCK. I reckon so. Anyways, I'm suited. These doughnuts must 'a' been good yesterday.

JOE. *(Reflectively)* S'pose they feel pretty bad to home?

TOM. Reckon they couldn't feel much worse.

JOE. *(With hesitation)* We been gone since Tuesday night an' it'll be Sunday when it's light. You don't reckon we ought to go back, do you?

TOM. That town won't see us again maybe in years. What we want to go back for?

JOE. *(Faintly)* I—I thought maybe we ought to go—to Sunday School.

TOM. Sunday School—— Well, I reckon not. Pirates don't go much on Sunday Schools.

JOE. Well, we needn't 'a' stayed to church. *(There is a pause)* Oh, boys, let's give it up. It's so lonesome. I want to go home.

TOM. Oh, no, Joe. You'll feel different when

daylight comes. Just think of the fishing that's here.

JOE. I don't care about fishing. I want to go home.

TOM. Oh, shucks, baby, you want to see your mother, I reckon.

JOE. Yes, I do want to see my mother. And I ain't any more baby than you are. *(He begins to sniffle.)*

TOM. Well, we'll let the cry-baby go home to his mother, won't we, Huck? Poor thing, does it want to go to see its mother, so it shall. You like it here, don't you, Huck? We'll stay, won't we, Hucky?

HUCK. *(Dolefully)* Yes, I reckon I'll stay if you will.

JOE. *(Moving off)* I'll never speak to you again, Tom Sawyer, not as long as I live. There, now!

TOM. Who cares? Nobody wants you to. Go 'long home and get laughed at. Oh, you're a nice pirate, you are. Hucky and me ain't cry-babies. We'll stay, won't we, Hucky? Let him go if he wants to. I reckon we can get along without him, p'r'aps.

HUCK. *(As JOE moves off)* I—I want to go too, Tom. It was getting so lonesome anyway, and now it'll be worse. Let's go too, Tom.

TOM. I won't. You can both go if you want to. I'm going to stay.

HUCK. Tom, I better go.

TOM. Well, go 'long. Who's hindering you?

HUCK. Tom, I wisht you'd come too. Now you think it over. We'll wait for you when we get to shore.

TOM. Well, you'll wait a blame long time, that's all. (HUCK *moves a step to follow* JOE HARPER. TOM *stands resolute, then suddenly gives it up and runs after the retreating* BOYS) Say! Wait! Wait! I want to tell you something. Hold on, Joe. Hold on, Hucky. I'll tell you what we'll do. If you'll wait till it's daylight, we'll all go back to the town together and look around and see what's going on. An' if you want to quit pirating an' go to Sunday School, Hucky and me won't hinder you. We'll just know you wasn't cut out to be a terror of the seas, or mebby we'll get up a regular robber gang instead, if you'll wait till 'bout ten o'clock. Is it a whack?

JOE. Yes, I'll stay, if we'll all go back together in the morning.

TOM. I meant to get back there about church time all along.

JOE. Then I'll go to sleep some more. But don't you go off again without waking me.

TOM. You go to sleep and me and Hucky will keep watch.

(JOE HARPER *crawls under the canvas.* TOM *and* HUCK *sit by the fire.* HUCK *lights his pipe and gives one to* TOM. TOM *smokes gingerly. The OWLS are heard hooting in the distance.*)

HUCK. *(After a silence)* Tom, do you reckon now that they've offered that thousand-dollar reward Muff Potter's got any chance?

TOM. Don't look as if he had. Everyone believes Muff done it, and they'll lynch him sure if he's ever brought back to that town. *(He whispers)* I heard 'em saying Injun Joe's sworn he'll fetch Muff Potter in and get that reward. He's been out with all the searching parties.

(As TOM *speaks a boat is seen crossing the open vista of moonlit river at the back. It is near the shore.* INJUN JOE *is alone in the boat. It hovers by the shore a moment and then passes on, crossing the stage at back from* L.U. *to* R.U. *The OWLS are heard again hooting nearer. A*

HOUND is heard baying faintly from the distance.)

HUCK. *(Who with* TOM *has not seen* INJUN JOE *pass in the boat)* That Injun devil will track him if anyone can.

TOM. *(After a pause)* Hucky, have you ever told anybody?

HUCK. Oh—'course I haven't.

TOM. Never a word?

HUCK. Never a solitary word, so help me. What makes you ask?

TOM. Well, I was afraid.

HUCK. Why, Tom Sawyer, we wouldn't be alive two days if that got found out. Injun Joe'd kill us as sure as my name's Huck Finn.

TOM. I reckon we're safe as long as we keep mum. But I hate to hear them abuse Muff when he never done that.

HUCK. Muff ain't no account, but then he hain't ever done anything to hurt anybody. He give me half a fish once when there wasn't enough for two, and lots of times he's kind of stood by me when I was out of luck.

TOM. 'Sh! What's that?

HUCK. *(Listening)* Sounds like—like hogs grunting. No. It's somebody snoring. Tom.

TOM. *(Listening)* Sounds like snoring. Where 'bouts is it, Hucky?

HUCK. Sounds like 'twas in the ha'nted house. Mebby it's old Jackson's ghost sleeping off a drunk.

TOM. Ghosts don't snore. Leastwise I never heard they did. Hucky, do you dast to look if I lead?

HUCK. I don't like to much, Tom, but l reckon I'll foller. *(They creep across and peer into the haunted house.)* Don't go no further, Tom.

TOM. Just a little ways. *(As they look into the*

haunted house, MUFF's *face appears in a broken window. The MOONLIGHT shines upon it.*) Oh, geeminy—it's him!

HUCK. Muff Potter. (MUFF *looks about him; sees* TOM *and* HUCK *in the shadow.*)

MUFF. Who's there? Don't shoot! I give myself up. I ain't a-going to make no fight. I don't want no more blood on these hands.

TOM. It's only us, Muff. Only Huck and me, and we won't tell.

MUFF. You—Tom Sawyer—Huck Finn! Ain't any others?

TOM. Joe Harper's asleep over in the tent, but I don't reckon Joe'd tell.

MUFF. Boys! Boys! It's you—it ain't no one else at all? Oh, boys, I been dreaming they was after me. I been on the island since Tuesday and I'm that starved and weak. I crept in here for shelter. Sing'ler I didn't see your camp. Mebby I was too weak to notice. You boys ain't afeared of me?

TOM. I reckon Ben Rogers might be, but Hucky and me ain't. You come on over to the fire and we'll give you what we've got.

MUFF. I'm that poorly an' low-spirited I ain't more'n able to crawl. Just been livin' on berries. You won't tell on me, boys? I know you won't, will you? Don't you wake Joe Harper or let on to him you've seen me. I don't care for myself much. It's Walt I'm a-thinking about. It's Walt that I've shamed and disgraced forever.

TOM. (*As they cross to the camp fire*) They've offered a reward of a thousand dollars to anyone who'll find you and fetch you in, an' they got a real detective from Saint Louis, too.

MUFF. A thousand dollars—and a Saint Louis detective—no, you don't say! My, boys, a thousand dollars is a heap of money, but you wouldn't let it tempt you to tell on old Muff and give him up to be hanged?

TOM. Nothing in this world won't ever make Hucky or me tell.

MUFF. What you boys doing here?

TOM. We're pirates.

MUFF. My, you don't say.

TOM. We been pirates since Tuesday.

MUFF. Land, it ain't possible. Trade brisk?

TOM. Only middlin'.

HUCK. *(Filling a pipe)* Want a smoke, Muff?

MUFF. My, Hucky, I should think I did. *(There is a pause.)* Well, boys, I done an awful thing—drunk and crazy at the time—— That's the only way I account for it, and now I've got to hide like a wolf in the woods with all them I knew best and loved most a-hunting me down or grieving and suffering and shamed for me. Come a little closeter to the fire. That's it. It's a prime comfort to see faces that's friendly when a body's in such a muck of trouble, and yourn are the first I've seen, and maybe they'll be the last friendly faces I'll ever see. Good friendly faces, good friendly faces. Shake hands, boys—if ye ain't afeared to do it—— Little hands and weak, but they've helped Muff Potter a power and they'd help him more if they could. What you think I'd better do, Tom?

TOM. You better put out down the river and never come back.

MUFF. I reckoned that was what I ought to do. But I ain't got no boat. I swum acrost to the bar when I come, an' I been afeared to go ashore an' find one. You ain't got no boat, I reckon?

TOM. Our boat got washed away. You better stay here quiet on the island. When it's light we're going back to town, and long about dusk Hucky and me'll hook a boat and drift down with the current and we'll take you in. Then you can put us ashore

somewheres near and go on down the river by yourself, and afore another morning you'll be miles and
miles away.

MUFF. I reckon that's about what I better do,
if you think you can get a boat and ain't afeared to
help old Muff. *(STEAMBOAT is heard on the
river.)*

TOM. Afeared—'tain't likely, is it, Huck?

HUCK. Not if you say it ain't. Tom, Lordy—
what's that?

MUFF. *(Listening)* Only the "Big Missouri"
paddling down the river. You'll see her lights soon
when she goes by. She'll be coming up again about
noon on Sunday. *(The LIGHTS of the steamboat
are seen passing in the distance.)*

TOM. There she goes now. *(He yawns)* My,
I'm most dead. I ain't slep' none tonight.

MUFF. Then you and Hucky'd better go to bed.
If you don't get no rest you'll be too tired to hook
that boat tomorrow. I'll keep watch.

TOM. You wake us as soon as it's light, won't
you, Muff? And say, Muff, if you hear anything,
the countersign is "blood."

MUFF. "Blood." I reckon I won't forget. I'll just
sit here and smoke my pipe till daylight comes.

TOM. Then we'll turn in. (HUCK *and* TOM *crawl
under the shelter* R.C. MUFF *smokes by the fire.
Presently he puts a stick on the fire. It blazes up.)*

MUFF. *(Softly)* Tom—Hucky—— *(He listens.
There is no answer)* No—fast asleep, I reckon.
They ain't got nothing a-weighin' on their hearts
like lead. *(He smokes in silence; nods over his pipe
by the fire; half sleeps. The MOONLIGHT fades
out. The scene is darker.* INJUN JOE *steals on at*
R.U. *He approaches stealthily, then lays his hand
upon* MUFF's *shoulder as* MUFF *drowses before the
fire.* MUFF *starts, looks up and sees him, the fire-
light on his face)* Injun Joe!

INJUN JOE. I reckon you didn't expect me, Pardner. But I suspicioned I'd find you here. I come in the night so's the whole town wouldn't be on my heels. I've heard talk of a posse coming to search the island at sun-up.

MUFF. At sun-up—then there ain't no chance for me.

INJUN JOE. I knowed if you was a-hiding here they'd corner you, so I come over to warn you. I've got a boat tied up in the bushes yonder. If you come with me you can slip away afore they're here.

MUFF. Oh, Joe, I'll bless you for this the longest day I live. *(He hesitates)* Tell me, Joe, honest now, old feller. Tell me how it was? I been studying and studying, but I can't recollect anything of it hardly. I wan't sober, an' my head was all in a muddle. I didn't know what I was doing. I never used a weapon in my life afore. Oh, ain't it awful, an' him so young and promising! It don't seem to me I could 'a' done it, Joe.

INJUN JOE. Look here, Pardner, that kind of talk won't wash. Didn't I tell you I seen you do it? Didn't they find your knife beside the door? I reckon you done it all right.

MUFF. *(On his knees before* INJUN JOE, *clasping his hands)* You won't tell on me, Joe—you wouldn't mislead me to get the reward—you wouldn't do that, would you, Joe?

INJUN JOE. No. You've always been fair and square with me, Muff Potter, and I won't go back on a pard. That's as fair as a man can say. *(Then with suspicion)* Who told you there was a reward offered? How'd you know about that?

MUFF. Tom Sawyer told me.

INJUN JOE. *(Suspicious)* That's a lie. Tom Sawyer's dead. He was drowned on Tuesday, along with Joe Harper and Huck Finn.

MUFF. No, he wasn't. Tom and Huck an' Joe

Harper's here. This is their camp. They've run off to be pirates.

INJUN JOE. Pirates, are they? They think they're dead back in the town. *(He takes a stealthy step toward the canvas)* They ain't said anything to you about me—nothing at all? *(WARN Curtain.)*

MUFF. *(Interposing)* Never a word, so help me.

INJUN JOE. I thought a minute ago you had notions in your head—— If I thought——

MUFF. *(Still between* JOE *and the sleeping* BOYS*)* Let 'em alone, Joe. They're asleep.

INJUN JOE. *(Drawing back)* I only thought they might split on ye. I didn't like the way they acted when I seen 'em afore Doc Robinson was found on Tuesday morning. Huck was hanging round late on Monday night. You don't suppose he seen anything?

MUFF. Nothing at all.

INJUN JOE. You don't reckon we better wring their necks an' drop 'em into the river? *(He moves threateningly toward the sleeping* BOYS.*)*

MUFF. *(Thrusting* INJUN JOE *back)* Not afore you wring mine! I ain't going to see no harm come to them boys.

INJUN JOE. *(For an instant his hand rests on the knife in his belt, then he draws back)* Fool! It's you that's taking the chances. This'll give the detectives a clue. We'd better be moving. You want to be miles below here afore daylight. It's lucky for you, Muff Potter, that Injun Joe's your pard.

(The TWO MEN *move off in the darkness toward the river. The* OWLS *hoot in the distance.)*

CURTAIN

ACT FOUR

SCENE II

The Village Street.

The Scene is the same as in Act I.

It is Sunday morning.

At rise, BEN, ALFRED, SID *and* AMY *are discovered, all in their Sunday clothes, hanging about the open door of the Church,* C.

BEN. I reckon 'most all the town'll be here to Tom's and Joe's funeral—and only last Sunday they was both here—and Tom hit me with a paper wad in Sunday School.

AMY. And Tom wore his new roundabout, and my mother says it's the very one he'll wear in Heaven, when he's an angel.

GRACIE. *(Who has entered at* L.U. *with a great bunch of bright flowers tied with twine)* My, don't they ever change up there?

AMY. My! Gracie, where'd you get all those flowers?

GRACIE. *(Displaying them proudly)* Begged the dahlias off Mis' Douglas, an' the pinks come out of Mrs. Jones's yard. I knocked but he wasn't to home, and I reached through the fence and got the flox out'n Mis' Morehouse's bed in her back yard. *(Looking into the Church door)* Ain't there no flowers at this funeral? My—I wouldn't 'a' treated Tom so.

BEN. But there ain't no corpses.

GRACIE. *(Haughtily)* No corpses! Amy Lawrence, how you talk. There's got to be corpses somewheres, or where's the sense in having a funeral— No corpses—it's scandalous.

AMY. Well, they ain't found 'em. They're a-lying stark and stiff somewheres, but we'll never see them again.

BEN. Do you remember, Sid, the last time we seen Tom—right the afternoon afore they went away? He come along and wanted to trade a piece of licorish and a fishline for a mouth-organ; an' I wouldn't—and I was a-standin' just so—just as I am now; and as if Alfred Temple was him—I was as clost as that—and he smiled—just this way—*(A sickly grin suffuses his face)* —and said he bet I'd wisht I had; and then something seemed to go all over me like—awful, you know—and I never onct thought what it meant. But I can see it plain now.

SID. *(With subdued pride)* I seen Tom last, I reckon. I was a-coming along the street and seen him climbing the fence right there; and he had a ham in one hand an' a box of lucifer matches in the other; and the light fell right on his forehead—and it seemed to shine—— I ought to 'a' knowed what to expect, but I never thought neither.

BEN. I got a white alley of his'n. I wouldn't take no money for that marble, now.

ALFRED. No, I reckon you wouldn't.

GRACIE. I got a piece of chewing-gum of Becky Thatcher's that Tom chewed once. I'll keep it just as long as I live to remember Tom by.

SID. Tom could run faster'n I could!

ALFRED. *(With pride)* Well, Tom Sawyer licked me once.

SID. *(Crushing him)* Oh—that ain't anything. Tom's licked 'most all the boys in town.

(The BELL is heard ringing in the Church, tolling for the funeral.)

GRACIE. My, ain't it solemn? Here's some of the mourners a-coming now—all in black, ain't they? Mis' Thatcher sent all the way to Constantinople in Union County for Mrs. Harper's dress. My, Amy, wouldn't you like to be a mourner, with everybody a-looking at you? There comes the Judge, and there's Becky. My, I reckon she feels bad about Joe.

AMY. I reckon she feels worse about Tom Sawyer.

GRACIE. *(Sadly)* Yes, I know they was engaged.

AMY. *(With great pride)* Me and Tom was engaged once!

(MRS. HARPER, MRS. THATCHER, BECKY, and JUDGE THATCHER enter from the HARPER gate and cross toward the Church door at C. AUNT POLLY enters from house R. with MARY and MRS. DOUGLAS, and advances to the Church door. The BELL tolls on.)

AUNT POLLY. *(To MRS. DOUGLAS)* There, I set all the night through—an' I know I never closed my eyes—dozed a little, maybe, but never really closed my eyes, and that cap's gone—Tom's cap! The last thing of his I'll ever have—— It's gone! It's gone!

MRS. DOUGLAS. It is sing'ler. You don't reckon Sid touched it?

AUNT POLLY. No, 'twas gone afore Sid woke.

MRS. HARPER. *(To AUNT POLLY, as they cross to*

the Church) It don't seem as if it can be true that I'll never see my Joe again.

AUNT POLLY. Oh, Sereny, I don't know how to give Tom up.

MRS. DOUGLAS. There, don't you give in or Mrs. Harper'll break right down. *(Exit* AUNT POLLY, MRS. DOUGLAS, MARY, SID, MRS. HARPER, MRS. THATCHER, BECKY, JUDGE THATCHER, *and* OTHERS *into the Church* C. *The* CHILDREN *follow them:* BEN, ALFRED, AMY, GRACIE.*)*

(WALTER *enters* R.U., *alone.* VILLAGERS *enter and pass into the Church. The street before the Church is deserted. The BELL tolls on a few strokes, and then stops ringing. As* ALL *exit into the Church,* TOM, JOE HARPER *and* HUCK *appear at* R.U. *and cautiously advance.)*

TOM. Hold on, Joe. We got all to go right together.

JOE. *(Looking about)* Ain't nobody round?

TOM. They're all in church.

JOE. *(Crossing)* Well, I'm a-going home.

TOM. Hold on, I tell you! Hark!

MR. SPRAGUE. *(From within the Church)*
      "Shall I be carried to the skies—
         On flowery beds of ease!
         Whilst others fight to win the prize,
         And sail thro' bloody—seas!"
Hymn Number Three Hundred and Forty-nine.

HUCK. What's that?

TOM. It's old Sprague linin' out the hymn. Say, boys, do you know what's goin' on in there?

JOE. No.

TOM. Do you, Huck?

HUCK. I reckon not.

TOM. It's a funeral!

JOE. My, you don't say!

HUCK. Whose?

JOE. Ain't old Mis' Miller, is it?

TOM. No, it ain't hers.

JOE. Nor Sally Magers?

TOM. No, I reckon it ain't Sally's.

JOE. By jingo, I wisht I knowed whose funeral it was.

TOM. I know. It's yours and Huck's and mine.

HUCK. Ourn! Lord! You don't say so.

JOE. Ourn! Why, Tom, we ain't dead. *(With sudden inspiration as the MUSIC swells in the Church, turning to the Church door)* Tom—you don't mean——

TOM. Yes, I do. This is our funeral, and it's the first one we ever had.

HUCK. My! You don't say so.

JOE. Oh, ain't it splendid! Are you sure and certain?

TOM. Hope I may die if I ain't. That's why I wasn't a-going to come back until this mornin'. Now ain't you glad you waited?

JOE. Say, ain't it grand! Won't Ben Rogers wisht he'd been along? Ain't it gay to be dead and be alive all the time? My, won't the boys be green? Oh, no, I reckon not! I guess there ain't anyone in this whole town that ain't a-thinkin' about us now.

HUCK. *(After a pause, as he listens near the door of the Church)* Where do you reckon they're going to bury us, Tom?

TOM. *(Before the Church door)* Oh, they'll put Joe in the Harper lot, and me in our lot.

HUCK. But I ain't got no lot!

TOM. Then they'll put you in the poor lot.

HUCK. I won't be put in no poor lot. I won't stand it.

TOM. How'll you help you'self?

HUCK. I'll up and ask the Widder Douglas to have me buried in her lot. *(Scratching his head)*

You don't reckon they'd be so ornery mean as to bury us very deep, do you, Tom?

Tom. How you talk! How can they bury us when they ain't got us?

Huck. Well, I wouldn't put it past 'em.

Tom. *(Still at door)* 'Sh! Old Sprague's naming our names. Want to look? *(The Boys line up on the steps before the Church, peering in over Tom's shoulder through a crack in the door.)*

Joe. Ain't that Ma there? My, she's all in black.

Huck. *(Near the door)* Just listen at that old liar. He ain't got no right to talk that way. What I ever done to him to have him a-calling me names like that?

Tom. *(Listening at the door)* That's just old pie 'longside what he said about you last night.

Huck. He'd better not blackguard me.

Tom. That's just what Widder Douglas said. She spoke right up an' said if you wasn't in hell this very minute it wasn't no fault of his.

Huck. My! Did the Widder speak up like that— for me?

Tom. She sassed him right there, afore his face, and Mis' Thatcher an' Mis' Harper an' Aunt Polly a-lookin' on, an' they couldn't stop her! An' you should 'a' seen her cry, an' carry on.

Huck. Did she carry on much, Tom?

Tom. Why, Huck, she carried on all the time, she felt just that bad. An' she said if she only had you back she wouldn't be so hard on you.

Huck. Did she say that, Tom, did she? *(He puts his knuckles in his eyes)* I'll stick to the Widder till I rot, Tom—and if I get to be a regular ripper of a robber, I reckon she'll be proud she snaked me in out of the wet.

Joe. Look out! They're a-coming! They're coming! *(As he speaks the People begin to come out of the Church, Aunt Polly leaning upon Judge*

THATCHER'S *arm, followed by* MRS. HARPER, MRS. DOUGLAS, *and* OTHERS.)

AUNT POLLY. *(Dropping the* JUDGE'S *arm as if she saw a ghost)* Tom Sawyer!

TOM. Ma'am!

AUNT POLLY. Tom Sawyer!

TOM. Yes'm!

AUNT POLLY. Tom Sawyer! You—you're alive —Tom—— You ain't dead and playing tricks on me! Tom! *(She seizes him, shaking him gently)* No. Flesh and blood! Oh, I thank the good Lord and Father of us all! I thank the Lord! *(She smothers* TOM *in her embrace, as* MRS. HARPER *and the* OTHERS *fall upon* JOE HARPER. HUCK, *much abashed, tries to sneak off* R.U., *unobserved.)*

TOM. *(As he sees* HUCK *neglected)* Aunt Polly, it just ain't fair. Somebody's got to be glad to see Huck, too.

MRS. DOUGLAS. And so they shall, poor motherless thing. I'm glad to see him, and I'm a-going to take him right straight home with me to Cardiff Hill.

HUCK. My, it's the Widder!

TOM. *(To* AUNT POLLY*)* We just been pirates on Jackson's Island all the time.

ALL. Pirates!

BEN. *(Eyeing* TOM *enviously)* I wisht I'd been a pirate, too.

GRACIE. *(Aside to* BECKY*)* Ain't Tom grand?

SID. *(Drawing a long breath)* My, I wisht I'd did what Tom done!

JUDGE THATCHER. *(Shaking his head and laughing with* MR. SPRAGUE*)* Sold, ain't we? Well, I reckon we won't be in such a hurry to bury them next time.

(Confused SOUNDS come from the distance. ALL

pause and listen, startled. Judge Thatcher *crosses toward* L.U.)

Voices. (*Off* L.U.) Lynch him! Lynch the murderer!

Mr. Jones. (Sheriff Jones *hurries on from* L.U.) They've got Muff Potter. Injun Joe found him on Jackson's Island before daybreak, took him off in a boat and landed ten miles below. (Tom *and* Huck *are startled by this announcement.*) They're bringing him now. Let all the women and children go home. I call on every man who respects the law to help maintain order. There ain't a moment to lose. (*Exit* Jones, L.U., *followed by* Judge Thatcher *and all the* Men. *As they exit* Walter *enters from Church. The* Women *and* Children *huddle before the Church.* Huck *exits* R.U.)

Voices. (*Off* L.U.) Lynch him! String him up to Doc Robinson's sign! Lynch the murderer!

Walter. (*As he enters*) Father! Oh, my God! My God!

A Voice. (*Off* L.U.) They're bringing him back to the scene of the murder.

Walter. Father! Father! They'll kill him!

Mary. (*Clinging to* Walter) Stop him! Don't let Walter go!

Mrs. Sprague. (*Re-entering* L.U.) Don't go, Walter! Stay here where you are. You can't do any good.

Mary. Walter! Don't look!

Voices. (*Off* L.U.) Lynch him! Lynch him! String him up!

Walter. Mary! Let me go! Let me go! Father! Father! (Walter *breaks from* Mary *and the* Others *and rushes off* L.U. Mr. Sprague *follows him.*)

Mrs. Harper. My, ain't it awful?

MRS. DOUGLAS. They'll get him away from Sheriff Jones!

AUNT POLLY. Where's Sid? Where's Tom? You children all of you go home right off.

MRS. DOUGLAS. Oh, God! They got him! Don't look! They'll kill him before our very eyes!

MRS. HARPER. Sheriff Jones and Walter've got him away.

MR. SPRAGUE. *(Re-entering* L.U.*)* Go home, go home, all of you. They're bringing him this way. Go home! Go home!

(CHILDREN *and* WOMEN *crowd into the Church in panic, as a mass of struggling* MEN *sweep on* L.U., *eddying like a whirlpool around and around* MUFF, SHERIFF JONES *and* WALTER, *struggling to tear* MUFF *from them.* WALTER'S *coat is torn.* MUFF *is in tatters. There is blood on his face, and on* WALTER'S. INJUN JOE *enters with them.*)

VOICE. *(From the struggling* MASS*)* Some of you get a rope! Let go of him, Mr. Jones! Go home, Walter. This ain't no place for you. Drag him off!

WALTER. Father! Father!

MR. JONES. Stand back in the name of the Law! Judge Thatcher, I call upon you to aid me!

JUDGE THATCHER. Make way for the prisoner! To the Church until we get aid! *(As he speaks* MR. JONES *and* WALTER, *with* MUFF, JUDGE THATCHER *and a crowd of* VILLAGERS, *attempt to reach the Church door. They are intercepted by the* MOB.*)*

VOICE. Don't let him get away! String him up! *(The* MOB *surges forward with* MUFF *in its midst, shaking as with a palsy.* MUFF *comes face to face with* INJUN JOE.*)*

INJUN JOE. *(To* SHERIFF JONES*)* I brought him in. I claim the reward.

MUFF. Joe, you promised me——

WALTER. Father! Tell them you didn't do it! For God's sake, Father, speak!

MUFF. *(Gasping for breath)* I—I—reckon I done it, Walt, but I can't remember how it was.

VOICES. You hear him! He's confessed!

MUFF. Don't let 'em kill me, Walt! I'm your father, ain't I, Walt? You won't go back on me.

WALTER. Oh, God!

VOICES. He's confessed! String him up! *(A rope is thrown over the* DOCTOR's *sign at* L. *The noose is fastened about* MUFF's *throat.)*

VOICES. Quick, men! Get it over! Up with him! Hoist away!

TOM. *(As a great groan goes up from the* ON-LOOKERS*)* Hold on, there! I reckon you better look out who you're hanging! Muff never done it! Muff's innocent!

INJUN JOE. *(Turning on* TOM*)* Innocent! What do you know about it?

VOICES. Innocent! He's guilty, and he'll swing for it!

TOM. *(Facing the* MOB*)* You was pretty certain about us being dead, wasn't you? But you ain't buried us yet, an' Muff ain't a-going to swing.

VOICES. String him up! What does Tom Sawyer know about the murder of Doc Robinson?

TOM. More'n I've told yet. I seen it. And if you don't believe me, ask Huck Finn. *(As he speaks* HUCK *re-enters* R.U., *breathless, with the shingle.)*

ALL. The boy's crazy!

TOM. *(With excitement, appealing to* AUNT POLLY*)* Oh, don't let 'em hurt Muff, and I'll tell.

AUNT POLLY. *(Advancing fearlessly and standing near* MUFF, *her hand upon his arm)* Take your time, Tom. Take your time. There's more'n one human life depending upon your words and I know you'll save 'em if you can. Take your time, and there ain't a mother's son here that'll ever look me in the face again if he raises his hand till he's heard ye!

TOM. Why, the night Doc Robinson was murdered Hucky and me was going to the graveyard to cure warts with a dead cat.

INJUN JOE. Bah!

TOM. After you and Sid got to sleep I heard Huck a-meowin' for me, so I raised the window an' got out on the roof an' slid down to the shed. Muff was a-settin' on Doc Robinson's steps—kind-a tipsy, an' he hove a rock at Huck an' says, "Dern that cat!" Right then Doc Robinson came back to the office, an' Huck and me clum up on the shed, 'cause we was afraid they'd see us an' tell, an' I'd git a licking. Then we seen the Doctor an' Muff begin to have words. Doc went into the office an' turned up the light, then he come back to send Muff away. He saw the knife in Muff's hand, an' Muff threw it down. Then they grappled. Just as Muff dropped the knife I saw Injun Joe standin' close to the Doctor's window, watching them—but they was too busy to notice him. When Muff grappled the Doctor, Injun Joe sneaked up closer, an' picked up Muff's knife. When the Doctor broke loose from Muff an' grabbed a scantlin' an' hit Muff an awful clip, Injun Joe jumped on him and jammed the knife into his side.

INJUN JOE. Hell! It's a lie! I'll be even with ye yet, damn ye all!

ALL. *(As* INJUN JOE *breaks through them)* Stop him! Stop the murderer! *(Quick as lightning,* IN-JUN JOE *springs away and is gone,* R.I. JONES *and* MEN *rush in pursuit. There is the report of a PISTOL. Re-enter* JONES)

JUDGE THATCHER. Sheriff Jones!

MR. JONES. *(Looking back)* Well, I reckon that case won't cost Marion County anything.

WALTER. Injun Joe——

MR. JONES. Dead. *(Looking at the pistol in his hand)* I'd never 'a' had the heart to hang a man.

HUCK. *(Advancing)* Say, if you don't believe what Tom says, looky here! *(He holds out the stained shingle.)*

TOM. My, Hucky! I forgot that!

HUCK. Well, I didn't! My thumb's sore yet!

TOM. We'd swore not to tell 'cause Injun Joe would 'a' drowned us if we had. But we just couldn't stand it to hear everybody abusing old Muff when we knowed he never done it.

HUCK. *(To* JUDGE THATCHER*)* I better give this to you.   *(WARN Curtain.)*

JUDGE THATCHER. *(Taking the shingle)* The Court accepts the evidence.

MUFF. Tom Sawyer! Why, what dern foolishness! Why, Tom! Oh—Walt! Walt! I've got another chance! I've got another chance!

TOM. We just come back to tell. Huck an' me an' Joe Harper wouldn't 'a' give up being pirates for no other reason in the world!

MARY. Oh, Tom! You've saved them both! You've saved them both!

WALTER. Father! Mary! Tom! *(He takes* TOM'S *hand and wrings it.)*

TOM. *(Squirming)* Here—look out—ouch! Let go! Say—Walt—I reckon you won't lick me for tearing your book about Anna Tommy, will you?

BECKY. But Tom didn't tear it—it was me. Oh, Tom, how could you be so noble?

TOM. Say, Muff, will you make me a big kite, some of these days, when me an' Becky's married?

MUFF. You married! What foolishness! How big a kite?

Tom. Oh, 'most as big a kite as the Widder's house on Cardiff Hill!

Aunt Polly. Laws-a-me! There never was any making of that boy out. Friends, I reckon when we're a-thinkin' our children's just playing old scratch, an' we'd like to tan 'em, the good Lord ain't a-forgettin' their tricks, and He just uses their devilment to work out His own good ends.

CURTAIN

"TOM SAWYER"

PROPERTY PLOT

ACT I

Books (Sid).
Leather-covered book (Walter).
Paper money (Robinson).
Teacup (Gracie).
Pail of whitewash and brush (Tom)
Rag on toe (Tom).
Pail (Sid).
Sewing-bag (Polly).
Thimble (Polly).
Spoons (Gracie).
Napkin (Gracie).
Apple (Ben).
Jewsharp (Huck).
Dead cat (Huck).
Kite (Muff).
Fishpole (Muff).
Corn-cob pipe (Muff).
Bladder (Joe Harper).
Corn-cob pipe and tobacco (Huck).
Matches (Huck).
Pansy (Becky).
Coins (Alfred).
Stick of wood.
Knife (Muff).
Stone.

Key (door L.I).
Tickets (Joe Harper).

ACT II

Book (Walter).
Broom.
Basket (Mary).
Books and slates (Children).
Peach (Tom).
Bucket of water.
Tin dipper.
Tickets (Tom).
Shingle.
Pin (Tom).
Flowers (Becky).

ACT III

Andirons.
Blue dishes (cupboard).
Cornucopias.
Wax flowers in glass case.
Dried grasses and berries.
Bric-a-brac.
Bible (table c.).
Doughnuts (cupboard).
Flatirons (Gracie).
Colander with doughnuts (Gracie).
Lamp (Aunt Polly).
Candle (table c.).
Cap (Mrs. Douglas).
Bark (Tom).

ACT IV

Bark (Huck).
Ham (Tom).

Doughnuts (Tom).
Corn-cob pipes (Huck).
Matches (Huck).
Flowers (Gracie).
Rope.
Pistol (Jones).
Shingle (Huck).

NOTE ON PRODUCTION

The Act II set can also be used for Act III if painted in neutral tones—the window R.C. becoming the door to kitchen and the teacher's plaform being replaced by mantel and fireplace.

"TOM SAWYER"

PUBLICITY THROUGH YOUR LOCAL
PAPERS

The press can be an immense help in giving publicity to your productions. In the belief that the best reviews from the New York papers are always interesting to local audiences, and in order to assist you, we are printing below several excerpts from those reviews.

To these we have also added a number of suggested press notes which may be used either as they stand or changed to suit your own ideas and submitted to the local press.

"——An ageless classic for children and grown-ups alike. ——Certainly it succeeds in being enjoyable, which is a lot. ——At its best when it deals with the children, with the high hopes, adventures and plans of red-blooded, ornery boys. The play most successfully evokes the spirit of the original story."—*"New York Times."*

Our local theatregoers will have the opportunity of seeing the living, breathing characters of Samuel L. Clemens' imperishable classic, "Tom Sawyer," as transferred to the stage by the master hand of Paul Kester, when the ————— Players present this charming play at the ————— Theatre on ————— evening.

Few Americans, or Europeans for that matter, have not revelled in this world-renowned story. If Samuel L. Clemens had written nothing else, his fame would endure on this one book alone.

Paul Kester, the dramatist, has contributed many notable successes to the American stage, among them being "When Knighthood Was In Flower," "Dorothy Vernon of Haddon Hall," "The Course of True Love," "Don Quixote," "Beverley's Balance," et al. "Tom Sawyer" is conceded to be the finest of his efforts, and the ———————— Players are congratulating themselves on having made so happy a selection for their next offering.

———————

In attempting to dramatize a great book, filled with character and incident, one is apt to become overwhelmed with an embarrassment of riches.

Perhaps the most notable example of discreet choosing and skillful blending is Paul Kester's dramatization of Samuel L. Clemens' immortal story, "Tom Sawyer." Mr. Kester's play starts out with the whitewashing of Aunt Polly's fence, and from then on all the most amusing and dramatic scenes in the book are woven together by Mr. Kester into a clear, consistent and highly enjoyable drama.

We meet all our old friends, from Aunt Polly to Injun Joe, not forgetting Tom and his friend, Huckleberry Finn and the rest of those highly imaginative, regular boys and girls with which Mr. Clemens peopled his book.

This most delightful of plays will be given at the ———————— Theatre by the ———————— Players on ———————— evening.

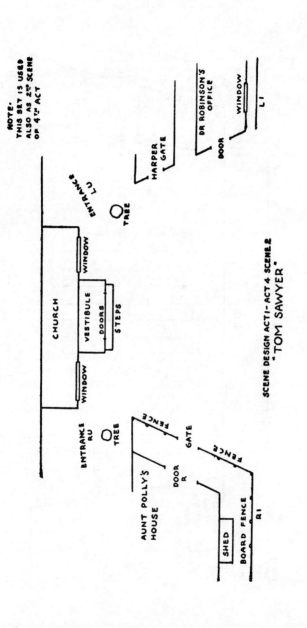

NOTE:
THIS SET IS USED ALSO AS 2ND SCENE OF 4TH ACT

CHURCH

WINDOW

VESTIBULE
DOORS
STEPS

WINDOW

ENTRANCE LU

TREE

ENTRANCE RU

TREE

HARPER GATE

DR ROBINSON'S OFFICE

DOOR

WINDOW

L1

AUNT POLLY'S HOUSE

DOOR R

FENCE

GATE

FENCE

SHED

BOARD FENCE

R1

SCENE DESIGN ACT 1 - ACT 4 SCENE 2
"TOM SAWYER"

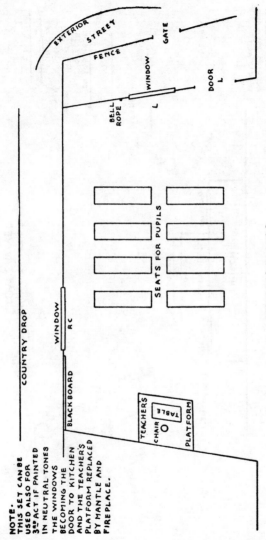

NOTE:
THIS SET CAN BE
USED ALSO FOR
3RD ACT IF PAINTED
IN NEUTRAL TONES
THE WINDOWS
BECOMING THE
DOOR TO KITCHEN
AND THE TEACHER'S
PLATFORM REPLACED
BY MANTLE AND
FIREPLACE.

COUNTRY DROP

EXTERIOR
STREET
FENCE
GATE
WINDOW
DOOR
L
BELL
ROPE
L

WINDOW
RC
BLACK BOARD

SEATS FOR PUPILS

TEACHER'S
CHAIR
O TABLE
PLATFORM

SCENE DESIGN ACT 2
"TOM SAWYER"

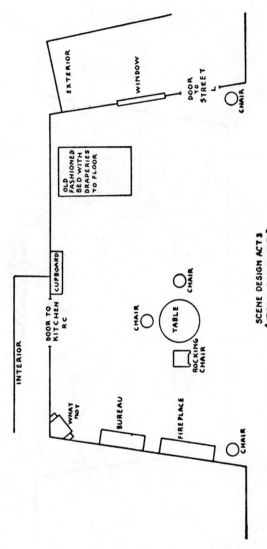

SCENE DESIGN ACT 3
"TOM SAWYER".

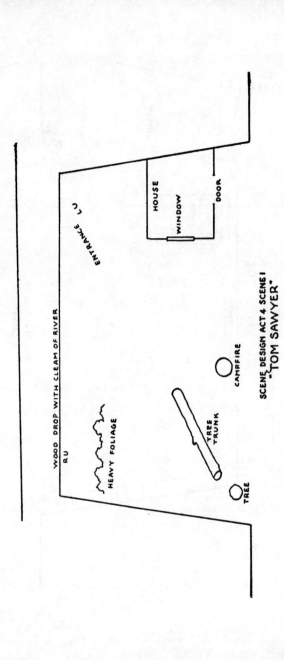

WOOD DROP WITH CLEAM OF RIVER

ENTRANCE

RU

HEAVY FOLIAGE

TREE TRUNK

CAMPFIRE

TREE

HOUSE

WINDOW

DOOR

SCENE DESIGN ACT 4 SCENE 1
"TOM SAWYER"

HOME-BUILT

Lighting Equipment
for The Small Stage
By THEODORE FUCHS

This volume presents a series of fourteen simplified designs for building various types of stage lighting and control equipment, with but one purpose in mind—to enable the amateur producer to acquire a complete set of stage lighting equipment at the lowest possible cost. The volume is 8½" x 11" in size, with heavy paper and spiral binding—features which make the volume well suited to practical workshop use.

Community Theatre
A MANUAL FOR SUCCESS
By JOHN WRAY YOUNG

The ideal text for anyone interested in participating in Community Theatre as a vocation or avocation. "Organizing a Community Theatre," "A Flight Plan for the Early Years," "Programming for People—Not Computers," and other chapters are blueprints for solid growth. "Technical, Business and Legal Procedures" cuts a safe and solvent path through some tricky undergrowth. Essential to the library of all community theatres, and to the schools who will supply them with talent in the years to come.

HANDBOOK

for

THEATRICAL APPRENTICES

By Dorothy Lee Tompkins

Here is a common sense book on theatre, fittingly subtitled, "A Practical Guide in All Phases of Theatre." Miss Tompkins has wisely left art to the artists and written a book which deals only with the practical side of the theatre. All the jobs of the theatre are categorized, from the star to the person who sells soft drinks at intermission. Each job is defined, and its basic responsibilities given in detail. An invaluable manual for every theatre group in explaining to novices the duties of apprenticeship, and in reassessing its own organizational structure and functions.

"If you are an apprentice or are just aspiring in any capacity, then you'll want to read and own Dorothy Lee Tompkins' A HANDBOOK FOR THEATRICAL APPRENTICES. It should be required reading for any drama student anywhere and is a natural for the amateur in any phase of the theatre."—George Freedley, Morning Telegraph.

"It would be helpful if the HANDBOOK FOR THEATRICAL APPRENTICES were in school or theatrical library to be used during each production as a guide to all participants."—Florence E. Hill, Dramatics Magazine.